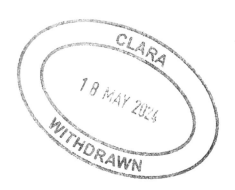

SCOUTING IN IRELAND

Scouting in Ireland

J. ANTHONY GAUGHAN

Kingdom
BOOKS

Typesetting and design by Susan Waine
Printed in Ireland by Colour Books Limited, Dublin
for

KINGDOM BOOKS
56 NEWTOWNPARK AVENUE • BLACKROCK
COUNTY DUBLIN • IRELAND

First published in 2006

British Library Cataloguing in Publication Data.
A catalogue record for this book is available from the British Library.

ISBN: 0 9524567 2 9

© J. Anthony Gaughan 2006

This book is set in 11 on 14 point Dante

Acknowledgements

I
N CONNECTION WITH the preparation of this book for publication I
wish to thank the staff of the National Library of Ireland, especially
Dónal Ó Luanaigh and Thomas Desmond.

I am grateful to the custodians of the institutions and to the individuals listed on pp. 164, 166, 168, 170-1 , particularly Comdt Victor Laing, Dónal Ó Luanaigh, and David Sheehy for allowing me to consult documents, manuscripts, papers and typescripts in their charge.

My thanks are due to all who gave me information and whose names appear on pp. 165, 172-3. In this regard Martin Burbridge, Walter Cullinane, Mrs Charlotte Fahy, Kiernan Gildea, John Graham, Dermot James, John O'Loughlin Kennedy, Matthew Kennelly, Malcolm Kincaid, Canon John MacMahon, Fr Colm Matthews, Séamus O'Connor, Stephen Spain and Michael Webb have been particularly helpful.

A special word of thanks is due to those the use of whose photos and pictures are acknowledged in the list of illustrations.

I am especially grateful to Dermot James and Donal McGahon, both of whom shared their extensive knowledge of Irish scouting with me. They took a close practical interest in all stages of the preparation of the book and to them as well as to Stephen Collins, Dr Marnie Hay, Canon Patrick Horgan and Maurice O'Connell, I am indebted for many helpful corrections and criticisms

I feel honoured in having the Foreword provided by the Chief Scout, Martin Burbridge, and the Envoi by Donal McGahon.

I am grateful to Eileen Francis for preparing the manuscript for publication and to Susan Waine for the design and layout of the book.

J. ANTHONY GAUGHAN
56 Newtownpark Avenue, Blackrock, County Dublin
1 MARCH 2006

'No man goeth about a more godly purpose than he who is mindful of the good upbringing not only of his own but of other men's children.'

SOCRATES

In grateful appreciation for the generosity of spirit and idealism of scout leaders, not least Michael Kennelly

Contents

LIST OF ILLUSTRATIONS

FOREWORD

Chief Scout, Martin Burbridge, and his wife, Eileen (Photo Neil Barry)

Chief Scout, Martin Burbridge,
and his wife, Eileen

Foreword

S COUTING IS A MOVEMENT of and for young people. The founder, Lord Baden-Powell, was very clear about that and he exhorted adults to find interesting, adventurous, challenging and fun ways to help young people to learn by doing, thereby developing themselves so as to be able to achieve their full potential.

Scouting has a value system embodying duty to God and good citizenship as espoused by the scout principles, the scout promise and the scout law. It is this value system that gives scouting its unique character and important role in the informal education of young people.

What you will read in the following pages relates the background and the wonderful achievements of individuals and groups involved over the last century in scouting in Ireland. It will certainly stimulate the imagination and reinforce one's gratitude to being privileged to be part of such a wonderful movement. It is this value system, together with the practice of Learning by Doing in small groups or patrols and the provision of opportunities for leadership and responsibility at a young age, that makes scouting unique.

Sincere thanks are due to all those who served scouting so well over very many years, for keeping the spirit and values of scouting alive and vibrant. As we stand near the beginning of the second century of scouting it is important to acknowledge the extraordinary achievements of those ordinary people who, working together, provided scouting for countless thousands of young people.

It is indeed an honour for Scouting Ireland to be charged with the task of carrying these values forward so that the young people of Ireland may enjoy their involvement in this wonderful movement. I believe that scouting is more relevant than ever to the development of young people to help them achieve their full potential and to imbue in them a sense of duty to God and of duty to others.

It is my fervent wish that all of the members of Scouting Ireland will continue to apply the scouting values, handed down by our predecessors, to all that they do so that the world will be a better place for all of God's creatures.

MARTIN BURBRIDGE
Chief Scout, Scouting Ireland
I MARCH 2006

PART I

Baden-Powell Scouts

Beginnings
Troubled Times
An Uncertain Era
Facing the Future

APPENDIX I: Religious Affiliations of Dublin
Association Groups 1955

CHAPTER ONE

Beginnings

BADEN-POWELL

ROBERT STEPHENSON SMYTH BADEN-POWELL is generally regarded as the founder of the boy scout movement. He was born in London on 22 February 1857 and was educated at Charterhouse public school. In 1876 he joined the British army and served in India, Afghanistan and South Africa. He was chief staff officer in a campaign in Matabeleland in 1896-7. In 1897 he completed an account of that campaign while stationed in Marlborough (now McKee) Barracks in Dublin. A few months later he was promoted to the command of the 5th Dragoon Guards in India.

In his autobiography he recalled his departure from Dublin:

> I arranged with my servant that I would slip away in the early morning before breakfast; and so, that it should not be noticed, he was to have a cab at the back door of my quarters, and get it loaded with all my luggage so I could nip away unseen.
>
> When all was ready I sneaked out the back door, there to find my cab, with the regimental sergeant-major sitting on the box and conducting the band...every man of my squadron harnessed in on long ropes, and the whole regiment there to see me out the barrack gate...
>
> My last glimpse of the barracks showed blankets being waved from every window, and all through the streets of Dublin went the mad procession which finally landed me at the station with a farewell cheer...

After serving in India Baden-Powell was transferred to South Africa. Following his courageous defence of Mafeking during the Boer War, he was promoted from colonel to major-general. Between 1900 and 1903 he organised the South African Constabulary. In 1904 he was appointed Inspector-General of Cavalry and for a period was stationed at the Curragh Camp, County Kildare.

THE ORIGINS OF SCOUTING

During the siege of Mafeking Baden-Powell or B-P, as he came to be known, had recruited the boys of the town as army messengers and had been impressed by their sense of responsibility. On his return to England B-P, referred to in the press as the 'Hero of Mafeking', was invited to take the salute at a march past at a Boys' Brigade rally by Sir William A. Smith. The Boys' Brigade was a Christian youth organisation founded by Smith at Glasgow in 1883 and involved a weekly meeting for drill and ancillary activities, a uniform and a Bible class on Sundays. Although B-P was impressed by the rally, he considered that the programme of the Boys' Brigade and similar organisations laid too much emphasis on drill and gymnastics and he devised a broader programme for incorporation by these organisations which would place greater emphasis on the individual and promote self-reliance.

In August 1907 he brought twenty boys – half from the Boys' Brigade and half belonging to no organisation, and one of whom was from Ireland – to Brownsea Island in Poole Harbour, Dorset, to test his programme of camping, games, nature study and self-reliance. The nine-day camp, during which the boys were organised into four 'patrols', was successful and from January 1908 onwards he had his programme printed, sold in six fortnightly parts and entitled *Scouting for Boys*. Existing youth organisations ignored B-P's programme, but young boys bought the magazines and started to form themselves into 'patrols' of 'scouts'. He went on a speaking tour organised by the Young Men's Christian Association (YMCA) to promote the programme. Suddenly B-P found he had a new youth organisation on his hands. In 1910 he retired from the army and devoted the rest of his life to travelling around the world visiting and encouraging one of the largest youth movements the world has known. He published four seminal books on various aspects of scouting which ran into numerous editions: *Scouting for Boys* (1908); *The Wolf Cub's Handbook* (1916); *Aids to Scoutmastership* (1919); and *Rovering to Success* (1922).

BEGINNINGS

As the movement's beginnings were spontaneous and lacking in organisation, it is not known who exactly could claim to be the first scouts or scout troops. However, within a year organisation was introduced, troops were registered, handbooks printed and a uniform designed. The girl guide movement originated in much the same way. It was promoted by the girls themselves in imitation of their brothers who were boy scouts. To give the movement some organisation B-P, with his sister, Agnes, provided a programme for the guides. After her marriage to B-P in 1912 Lady Olave Baden-Powell became involved in the movement, became chief commissioner in 1916 and Chief Guide of the movement in 1918.

The first handbook was based on *Scouting for Boys* which had been published by B-P in 1908. This set out the aim of the movement, which was to train boys in the essentials of good citizenship. It was to be achieved by stimulating self-expression and a desire to learn on the part of the boy rather than encouraging his passive reception of instruction. The movement was to be open to all, regardless of class, race, colour, creed or political affiliation. Honour was made the high ideal for boys. The scout law on which the movement was based was binding on every scout who, on joining, made a promise on his honour to do his best to do his duty to God and his country, to help other people at all times and obey the scout law.

SCOUTING BECOMES INTERNATIONAL

The first countries outside Britain to establish scouting were those which were part of the British empire. Scouting began in Australia, Ireland, Malta, New Zealand and South Africa in 1908. In Canada and India it was established in 1909. In the US, the Woodcraft movement already existed, inspired and led by Ernest Thompson Seton. Its programme was based on the lore and outdoor craft of the various Native tribes. This organisation was subsumed into the Boy Scouts of America, which derived its inspiration from B-P. Seton then wrote the first handbook for the Boy Scouts of America Association, which was incorporated in 1910 and was granted a federal charter in 1916. By the end of 1910 over 100,000 scouts had been registered worldwide. In 2004 the organisation had 28 million members and its central office was in Geneva in Switzerland.

BEGINNINGS IN IRELAND

As elsewhere the beginnings of the scout movement were spontaneous in Ireland, where it was claimed that a troop formed in Bray, County Wicklow, was one of the first in the world. During the first months no records were kept and eventually there were five different associations supervising troops in Dublin city and county. Notwithstanding this early confusion, it is known that the first scout in Dublin was enrolled on 15 February 1908 in the Wolf Patrol of the 1st Dublin troop by the scoutmaster Lieutenant R.P. Fortune, Dublin Squadron, Legion of Frontiersmen. Also it is recorded that the 2nd Dublin troop was set up on 21 February 1908 by Bernard C. Cunningham from the Kylemore Cricket and Hockey Club and members were formally enrolled on 2 March at 5 Upper Camden Street. In 1909 there was a troop associated with Marlborough (now McKee) barracks, consisting of boys whose fathers were serving in Irish regiments of the British army. The uniform was a khaki shorts and shirt and what became known as a broad-brimmed B-P hat. The shorts and hat continued to be required parts of the uniform until 1952.

EARLY SUCCESS

The earliest extant minute book of the organisation started with a meeting of the Dublin Central Committee on 14 October 1909 but the *Evening Mail* on 20 March 1909 reported that: 'The boy scout movement in Dublin seems to be gaining ground rapidly, the number of lads that turned out on St Patrick's day being upwards of 500'. It listed the troops and their scoutmasters who had assembled at St Stephen's Green and described their subsequent hike and campfire at Three Rock mountain. The *Evening Mail*, with Bernard C. Cunningham as the first compiler of scout news, was to provide a treasure trove of information on the progress of the movement. In its issue of 8 January 1910 the following appeared:

> By the very kind permission of the editor of the *Evening Mail*, the boy scouts organisation in Dublin has been granted space where all news concerning the movement can be published.
>
> There are at present in Dublin twenty-nine troops, comprising 700 officers, non-commissioned officers and scouts. The boy scout is taught everything that the imagination of a boy can conceive. He is taught rowing, shooting, riding, tracking, pioneering, signalling, gymnastics, ambulance work, fire-lighting, cooking and one hundred and one other things that every boy loves to have a hand in. In summer he goes to camp and in a number of instances he has weekend camps all through the season.

By this time a central committee had been set up. Its role was to supervise the Dublin district associations which managed scouting in (1) North City and County, (2) South City and (3) South County.

In late 1907 and early 1908 boys in the Belfast area, inspired by B-P's exploits and writing on scouting, formed themselves into scout patrols. These emerged within existing youth organisations such as the Boys' Brigade and the YMCA. Meetings of the 1st Belfast troop were held from March 1908 onwards. Soon afterwards the 2nd Belfast was formed. It was also known as 'the Earl of Shaftesbury's Own'. During the next five years more than a score of troops were established in Belfast and other troops were formed elsewhere in Ulster.

In 1909 B-P headquarters in London appointed the earl of Shaftesbury the first commissioner for Ireland and Viscount Massereene and Ferrard the first commissioner for the province of Ulster. By 1910 the number of local associations which had been set up to supervise troops in Ulster had reached twelve.

VISITS BY CHIEF SCOUT

In 1910 B-P inspected the Dublin scouts at the staff gymnasium, Portobello (now Cathal Brugha) Barracks. The event was organised and supervised by officers of the Wiltshire regiment. He also visited Belfast and Cork. In March 1911 the Chief Scout was back again to inspect his Dublin scouts. This time the venue was the gymnasium of the Royal Hibernian Military School. In April he was in Belfast to review 800 scouts from Belfast, Bangor and Holywood. Political tension was building in Ulster owing to the anti-Home Rule movement. The Chief Scout in his report on his visit in the *Headquarters Gazette* of June was at pains to point out that the B-P organisation was not a military movement and did not interfere in any way with religion but 'gives priest or pastor a better hold over the more thoughtless of his lads and it is a self-governing movement in its own locality'. In July about 500 Dublin scouts and 200 more from Belfast, Dundalk, Kildare and Wicklow took part in a scout parade during a Royal garden party in the Phoenix Park on the occasion of the visit of King George V. In those early years church parades were occasionally held to the various British garrison churches. Each October a census of membership was taken and in 1911 there were some 900 members in Leinster alone, with troops being started all over the country.

Following his visit to Ireland in 1911 the Chief Scout also stated in his report:

> We want the movement in Ireland to run itself for Ireland. The scheme now being carried out is under an Irish Chief in Lord Shaftesbury, each province will have its own commissioner, with county commissioners and local associations under them, the headquarters to be in Dublin.

In 1912 the 12th Earl of Meath replaced Shaftesbury as commissioner for Ireland. In the same year the Belfast association opposed the formation of

an Irish Boy Scout Association and insisted that each province be administered by its own commissioner. Shortly afterwards the earl of Leitrim was
appointed to that end.

INVOLVEMENT OF ANGLO-IRISH ARISTOCRACY

From the outset members of the Anglo-Irish aristocracy were particularly
supportive of the B-P scouts. In 1911 the 3rd North Dublin troop became
'Lord Holmpatrick's Own' and was given camping facilities in his estate at
Abbotstown, Castleknock. In the following year the 8th Dublin, 'Earl of
Pembroke's Own', were given camping facilities at Powerscourt,
Enniskerry. By that time the 8th Viscount Powerscourt was chief commissioner for Leinster and had begun a long and close association with the
movement. The 12th Earl of Meath provided camping facilities at
Kilruddery and in July 1913 travelled to inspect the Irish contingent at a rally
and exhibition at Birmingham attended by 30,000 'from all parts of the
empire'. Subsequently, on 1 July 1920, he was the first Irish scout leader to
complete the scoutmaster's course at Gilwell Park, then a fifty-three-acre
training centre on the edge of Epping Forest, near London. Sir Stanley
Cochrane, who was for some years president of the Dublin Boy Scouts'
Association, made his residence and estate at Woodbrook, near Bray, available for the troops in County Wicklow. The 9th Baron Talbot provided
camping facilities on his estate at Malahide to local B-P scouts in the 1950s.
The 24th Dublin troop was named 'Pack-Beresford's Own' after a prominent County Carlow Anglo-Irish family with branches in Counties Down
and Dublin. In Ulster the leading citizens of Belfast, as well as landed gen-
try, not least Sir Robert Kennedy of Cultra Manor, Holywood, County
Down, were equally supportive of the B-P scouts.

FIRST SEA SCOUTS

In September 1912 the 1st City of Dublin Sea Scouts was registered and was
soon joined by the 2nd City of Dublin Sea Scouts, both founded by the then
Captain R. P. Fortune. However, it is generally agreed that sea scouting had
begun in Ireland as early as 1910 and in the early summer of 1912 a sea scout
troop had been formed in Bray, County Wicklow, with Reverend Mr Lefroy
as scoutmaster. In 1913 sea scouts from the 1st Dublin attended a scout rally
and exhibition in Birmingham and won a prize for all-round seamanship.
The prize was presented by B-P's brother, Warington Baden-Powell, who
had published *Sea Scouting and Seamanship for Boys* in 1912. For many years
the sea scouts managed their own affairs but eventually they were merged

with the Dublin Boy Scouts' Association. In September 1913 the numerical strength of the Dublin scouts stood at 1,000 and the number of scouts throughout Ireland was estimated at over 20,000.

Throughout 1913 scout activities were unaffected by the General Strike and Lock-out. The only effect which the consequent 'disturbances' had on the movement was a directive issued to Dublin city troops on 13 September 1913 not to wear uniform on parades. From 1914 onwards the Dublin sea scouts organised an annual regatta, at which sometimes as few as two and sometimes as many as ten troops competed for the Wood-Latimer trophy.

CHAPTER TWO

Troubled Times

W ITH THE OUTBREAK OF WAR the Dublin City and county associations of Boy Scouts took immediate steps to seek ways and means of helping with the war effort. The *Evening Mail* of 29 August 1914 gave an outline of the activities in which scouts became involved.

It is somewhat interesting to note the active part our boy scouts of the city of Dublin are filling at the present crisis. Their duties are principally concerned with telephone and message work and they have already been congratulated by the staff at headquarters for their energy and zeal.

It should be borne in mind that these boys are carrying out duties specially laid down by the military authorities.

Their hours of duty are from 10 a.m. to 1 p.m., and from 2 p.m. to 6 p.m. each day and from 10 a.m. to 1 p.m. on Sundays until their services are dispensed with. In conveying telegrams and large consignments of letters, some of the Scouts have been found invaluable, especially in the conveyance of orders to important centres in Dublin.

In connection with this work, the Commissioners of National Education, have been, we understand, approached with a view of lessening the hours of attendance of a large number of boys in school, and it is hoped that the commissioners will see their way to afford every facility possible to those lads who are anxious to help their country in the hour of need.

Following on the suggestion of Sir Robert Baden-Powell, Chief Scout, the County of Dublin Boy Scouts will have a big job before them with regard to protection of railway bridges, tunnels, telegraphs, water supplies, etc., and many other useful duties which are set out in his comprehensive announcement.

The sea scouts are also in the position of affording valuable assistance in their sphere of action. It is to be hoped that the portion of the appeal especially addressed to ex-scouts will bring forth a hearty response, and that their exceptional experience will be ungrudgingly placed at the disposal of their country's defenders.

The educational authorities granted permission to the boys engaged in official duties to count the work with the military as equivalent to 'school attendance' and by 16 August 120 scouts were regularly thus engaged. At a general inspection of Dublin scouts in the Phoenix Park in November the Marquess of Aberdeen, Lord Lieutenant of Ireland, thanked them for 'the valuable work' they were doing 'during the time of the national crisis', and commended them for living up to their motto 'Be Prepared'.

The scouts in Belfast were as committed to supporting the war effort as their comrades in Dublin. Some were involved in rifle drill and firing practice as part of their training in a 'Scouts' Defence Corps for Home Services'. Others did spells of duty: coast-watching; as hospital orderlies; and in fire stations. They also raised funds to provide a rest centre for soldiers near the front in France which became known as the 'Belfast Scouts' Hut'. In 1918 they launched a 'garden plots scheme' to encourage people to produce more food. As with the Dublin scouts, many of the Belfast leaders and scouts who enlisted for the war did not survive it.

THIRD VISIT OF CHIEF SCOUT

The Dublin scouts received a third visit from the Chief Scout in August 1915. For the occasion the annual rally and general inspection was held in Lord Iveagh's gardens near St Stephen's Green. After the usual displays by various troops there was a march past. On the reviewing stand were the Chief Scout, referred to in press reports as Lieutenant General Sir Robert Baden-Powell, KCB, a large number of army officers, led by General Friend, CB, commander of the British forces in Ireland, and other dignitaries. Earlier on the same day the Chief Scout had inspected members of the Dublin companies of the girl guides, numbering 200, in Merrion Square. B-P reported on his visit to Ireland in the Scouts *Headquarters Gazette* of September 1915. After a patronising remark about religious and political differences in Ireland he expressed his satisfaction that these had been put aside and Irishmen had 'joined their forces with those of the empire'. He selected for special praise sea scouts who were serving as signallers on 'His Majesty's Ships' and scouts who had been doing orderly work in military headquarters. Before the end of the war in 1918, apart from the scouts who provided services at military and naval installations in the Greater Dublin area, some 600 Dublin scouts, almost half the total number, many of them leaders, enlisted in the army and navy and seventy-six lost their lives in the war.

The Chief Scout also visited Belfast, where he reviewed a rally of Ulster scouts at Cliftonville Football Grounds. Among the 1,250 on parade were representatives from the Belfast troops and thirty-three other troops from across the province. B-P acknowledged the war efforts of the scouts on the home front as well as those who had joined the armed forces. In his report on the visit he noted that the only sea scouts were in Dublin at Kingstown. This prompted the formation of the 1st Belfast sea scouts in 1919. However, sea scouting was to become popular in Northern Ireland only after World War Two.

EASTER RISING

The Rising of Easter Week 1916, the consequent imposition of martial law and the executions that followed had their repercussions on the Dublin boy scouts. Most troops were in camp for the weekend and some scouts had difficulty in returning to their homes in the city. Directives to groups with regard to camping and the wearing of uniforms varied but generally urged caution in these matters. The scout troops involved in war service were instructed to carry on as usual. Occasionally scouts were left in no doubt as to how some of their fellow-citizens regarded their close association with the Crown forces. In the wake of the Rising the log book of the Port of Dublin Sea Scouts reported:

> No less than twenty attempts were made to rob, wreck or burn the hut. On one occasion the boys were made to line up against the wall and were threatened they would be shot if they attempted to move. In the meantime, boxes, drawers and cupboards were ransacked, the telescope was taken away and windows were broken. The raiders eventually left with these final orders: 'If any of you leave this hut within fifteen minutes after we have gone, you will be shot'. Immediately the raiders left the scouts were out in time to see them drive away, but smoke was billowing out from the lower windows of the coastguard station. The scouts dashed up and entered the building just in time to stamp on a lot of straw, sprinkled with petrol, which had been strewn about the floor and which was already alight.

DUBLIN BOY SCOUTS ASSOCIATION

Towards the end of 1916 the Dublin City and Dublin County associations were amalgamated to form the Dublin Boy Scouts Association, which was subsequently to remain the governing body for the organisation in the area. The two associations had had responsibility for eleven and eighteen troops respectively. An attempt in 1917 to renumber troops failed because of determined opposition. The most serious challenge which the leadership facing at this time was the serious fall in membership as many scout leaders and hundreds of scouts had joined up to fight in the war.

PUBLICATIONS

In 1917, owing to the war shortages, the *Evening Mail* was no longer able to provide space for 'Scout notes'. This prompted some Dublin scouts to publish a quarterly *Scout News*. In March 1918 this was replaced by a *News Sheet* which was issued to scoutmasters throughout the country from this time on except during World War II. In the meantime in 1920 Lord Meath had launched a short-lived *Irish Scouts Gazette* to cater for the movement in Ireland and as a supplement to the *Headquarters Gazette*. Beginning in May 1920 the Belfast boy scouts published the *Belfast Scout News*, which was replaced in 1924 by *The Ulster Scout*.

SCOUTING AS USUAL AND ECHOES OF THE WORLD WAR, 1917–20

In 1917 Dublin scouts organised a swimming gala which was to become part of their annual programme. Activities in 1918 continued to be influenced by the war. In July the scouts were addressed by the Lord Lieutenant, Field Marshal Viscount French. In 1919 a scout display was organised in the Theatre Royal. This was addressed by the 8th Viscount Powerscourt and the Lord Chancellor and it was to become an annual event. That year also saw the formation of the first troops of Irish rover scouts in Dublin and in Belfast, that is, scouts with an age range from seventeen upwards. In May, at the suggestion of B-P, a memorial service was held in Christchurch Cathedral for all scouts who had lost their lives in the war. Later, Dublin scouts paid tribute to their own fellow-scouts when attending a service at which a memorial was unveiled in St Patrick's Cathedral. From 1919 onwards Irish troops were registered at the B-P headquarters in London. In 1920, 8000 scouts attended the 1st World Scout Jamboree at Olympia, London. The Irish contingent consisted of 220 scouts from the greater Belfast area, together with 280 scouts representing twenty-one Dublin and two County Wicklow troops. Among the 360 sea scouts attending the jamboree were twenty-nine from the 1st Dublin Sea Scouts who were accommodated on board the training-ship *Northampton*. In a note to the 12th Earl of Meath, B-P conveyed his pleasure at the splendid turnout of the Dublin and Belfast scouts, especially 'knowing the great difficulties with which you have to contend in Ireland...'

WAR OF INDEPENDENCE, 1919-21

The difficulties referred to by B-P arose from the war of independence. IRA activists and the British forces were matching atrocities and this made normal scouting activity well-nigh impossible. Some scouts in uniform were attacked and there is evidence that some weekly meetings and meeting places had to be given discrete police protection. Moreover parents were loath to allow their children on the streets by day or night because of the danger in which they could find themselves. By 1921 early curfew regulations, part of a martial law regime, effectively ended the holding of meetings. The earl of Bandon, Commissioner for Munster, was abducted by the IRA but survived the experience. Sir Arthur Vicars was not as fortunate. He was the driving-force behind and secretary of the Listowel troop. In April 1921 he was shot as a spy by the IRA and his residence, Kilmorna House, was destroyed. Fortunately, a planned assassination of the earl of Meath at this time, because he was allegedly recruiting for the British army from the B-P scouts, was not attempted.

QUINTESSENTIAL IMPERIALIST

Whatever about the earl of Meath's role as a recruiting officer for the British army, his credentials as an imperialist were second to none. In 1902 he founded the Empire Day Movement, which, on 24 May, anniversary of Queen Victoria's birthday, celebrated 'Empire Day'. An *Empire Catechism* was published to help scouts to celebrate the day appropriately. On 11 May 1921 the earl of Meath sent the following 'Empire Day message' to G. S. Childs, district scoutmaster, County Wicklow association:

> It gives one great pleasure to learn that the Bray scouts, guides, wolf cubs and brownies are holding a special parade on Empire Day, 24 May, that General Crosbie has promised to inspect them and that every scout and guide will renew his or her three-fold promise on the occasion.
>
> I am especially pleased to hear this last piece of information, for I feel it is most important in these troublous times that we should support and

strengthen ourselves and each other by the remembrance of the solemn promises we all took when we entered our world-wide organisation and by renewing our vows in the presence of each other. It will be of interest to you and your brother scouts and girl guides to know that Sir Robert and Lady Baden-Powell have returned from their distant travels in the East and report the spread of the movement in India, Ceylon, Burma, Palestine and Egypt...

CIVIL WAR, 1923–4

With the withdrawal of British forces from twenty-six counties of Ireland hostilities broke out between those who supported and those who opposed the Anglo-Irish Treaty . In 1922 the earl of Meath, who was to be the last All-Ireland commissioner, reported to London on the continuing difficulties this presented to scouting and the Irish commissioners were directed 'to suspend public scout activities in Ireland until they received further instruction from imperial headquarters'. The B-P scouts were not deflected from showing their deep attachment to Britain. In October they were well represented at a huge scout rally at Alexandra Palace, London. The occasion was described as a 'posse of welcome' to the Prince of Wales on his return from one of his overseas tours. In 1923 the prominent unionist, Lord Glenavy, then chairman of Seanad Éireann, was invited to address the annual scout display in the Theatre Royal. Then in 1924, while about 400 scouts from Belfast, Bray, Cork, Dublin, Letterkenny and Limerick attended the Imperial Scout Jamboree at Wembley, London, just sixteen took part in the 2nd World Scout Jamboree at Ermelanden in Denmark.

B-P SCOUTS IN NORTHERN IRELAND

In the meantime, by virtue of the Government of Ireland Act of December 1920, the six counties of Ulster – now named Northern Ireland – continued to be an integral part of the United Kingdom. In 1923, on the recommendation of the earl of Meath, the Ulster Provincial Council became the 'duly constituted authority for the Ulster division of the Boy Scouts Association'. Subsequently a provincial commissioner was appointed to exercise this authority. From the 1920s onwards the B-P scouts flourished across Northern Ireland and were prominent in the ceremonies marking the important and festive events of the province.

CHAPTER THREE

An Uncertain Era

A T ORGANISATIONAL LEVEL the B-P scouts in the twenty-six counties were not substantially affected by the new constitutional relationship between the Irish Free State and Great Britain. The Irish Free State had elected to remain in the Commonwealth so the connection with imperial headquarters could be maintained and 'Southern Ireland' was administered as if it were a county in Great Britain. Subsequently an Irish Free State Scout Council was set up to deal with the operation of the organisation within its jurisdiction. The new status of the Irish Free State B-P scouts was recognised at the jamboree in Wembley in 1924 when they were accommodated in a portion of the camp for 'scouts who had come from distant parts of the empire'. In their display in the stadium they exhibited a hurling match, Irish dancing and music on the uillean pipes.

ANXIETY ABOUT THE FUTURE OF IRISH B-P SCOUTS
From the mid-1920s onwards some leaders became anxious about the future status of the Irish B-P Scout Association in their newly independent country. The political environment in which the scouts had been introduced to Ireland was such that it was natural that leaders and members were almost entirely Protestant, unionist and middle-class. The B-P scouts had also had close relations with the British forces in the country, with regard to leaders, meeting-places and rallies. Notwithstanding occasional protestations to the contrary, the ambience surrounding B-P himself and B-P scout headquarters in London sought to emphasise loyalty to the British empire. B-P scouts had flourished in Ulster and in that part of the rest of Ireland where traditionally are found some of the highest levels of loyalty to Britain and the British empire. Thus by 1926 there were about thirty well established troops in Dublin city and Counties Dublin and Wicklow. But elsewhere, apart from Cork, Belfast and surrounding districts, Abbeyleix and Carlow it had not been possible to sustain troops for significant periods.

FOUNDING OF CATHOLIC BOY SCOUTS OF IRELAND, 1926-7

The anxieties of leaders about the future of their association in the Irish Free State were exacerbated by the establishment of the Catholic Boy Scouts of Ireland (CBSI) in 1926-7. B-P scouts saw the new organisation as a serious challenge to efforts to encourage more Catholics to join their association. Perhaps to counter the influence of the CBSI in this regard a member of the new Seanad Éireann, Major General Sir William Hickie, was invited in July 1926 to take the review at Lord Iveagh's gardens of the annual rally of the Dublin city and county scouts. He was the first Catholic to do so and emphasised in his address that he wished there were 'more scouts in the Free State and that it was more generally recognised that the movement was non-political and non-sectarian'. The following year another Catholic member of the Seanad, General Sir Bryan Mahon, was on the reviewing stand. In the meantime, in December 1926, at the annual scout display in the Theatre Royal the earl of Meath also emphasised that the scout movement was 'non-military, non-political and non-denominational'. Notwithstanding anxieties about the future, Lord Powerscourt, chief commissioner of the B-P scouts in the Irish Free State, in a letter to a scoutmasters' conference towards the end of 1926 stated that he hoped that to the CBSI 'the hand of friendship would never be withheld by a B-P scout'.

LAST VISITS OF CHIEF SCOUT, 1928 AND 1929

By the 1920s many of the inter-troop competitions were held each year. 525 Irish scouts, under the leadership of the 8th Viscount Powerscourt, participated in the 3rd World Scout Jamboree at Arrowe Park, Birkenhead, in 1929. The national flag was flown over the Irish Free State camp and was carried in the general march past. At that jamboree the visiting Australian scouts wore woggles on their scarves and subsequently woggles became popular with scouts everywhere.

The highlight of the 1920s were the last visits of the Chief Scout. By this time B-P was at the height of his popularity. At the 1st World Scout Jamboree at Olympia in London in 1920, which was attended by a contingent of more than 230 from Ulster, he had been acclaimed as 'Chief Scout of the World'. For twenty years he had travelled the world visiting and encouraging scouts everywhere. In 1928 there were over two million scouts in forty-two countries. Lady Baden-Powell had become Chief Guide in 1918 and throughout the world guides were becoming as numerous as the boy scouts. During his visit to Dublin in 1928 B-P reviewed 2,000 guides at Lansdowne Road and spent a day inspecting 500 scouts at their camp sites in the Powerscourt Demesne at Enniskerry. He later reviewed scouts in Cork.

His visit to the Powerscourt Demesne was not without incident. Percy Scott, who for many years was camp chief at the Demesne and served later as honorary general secretary, recalled how a planned welcome for the Chief Scout went awry. The scouts were hidden in the sunken road opposite Powerscourt House. When B-P and Lord Powerscourt arrived in a horse-drawn carriage the order was given and the scouts appeared over the sunken wall cheering wildly. The horse took fright and bolted. After the horse was brought under control B-P and Lord Powerscourt were much shaken.

In 1929 B-P and Lady Baden-Powell visited Northern Ireland where a joint rally of 11,000 scouts and guides greeted them at Balmoral Show Grounds in Belfast.

IRISH FREE STATE SCOUT COUNCIL

In 1930 the Irish Free State Scout Council was set up. Its objects were to 'promote scouting in the Irish Free State and to arrange for harmonious cooperation with existing organisations for boys'. In 1931 a scout fair in the Mansion House was added to the annual programme. This was opened by the Lord Mayor of Dublin, Senator Alfred (Alfie) Byrne. In July Irish Free State scouts represented the British Isles at Sweden's national jamboree at Helsingborg. In the same month thirty Dublin Rover scouts attended the 1st World Rover Scout Moot at Kandersteg, Switzerland. In 1935 twelve Dublin Rover scouts participated in the 2nd World Rover Moot at Ingaro, Sweden. By 1935 there were 800 Rover scouts in Northern Ireland and they were also represented at the 2nd World Rover Scout Moot.

The depressed economic conditions of the 1930s did not unduly affect scout programmes. Dermot James's history of the 33rd Dublin (Sandford) Scout Group provides an insight into the activities of Dublin scouts at that time. Apart from routine activities, this troop took part in inter-troop competitions, the annual scout sports, swimming gala and rally, established a permanent week-end camp site on Powerscourt Demesne, held their annual camps in England and Wales and had members in the Irish scout groups which attended the 4th and 5th World Scout jamborees, at Godollo in Hungary in 1933 and at Vogelensang in Holland in 1937. At these jamborees Ulster was also represented by substantial contingents.

THE ÉIRE SCOUT COUNCIL, 1937

After the enactment of the State's new constitution, in 1937, when the title 'Irish Free State' was replaced by 'Éire', the Irish B-P Scout Association's title was altered to 'The Éire Scout Council'. The Council continued to be self-governing but the connection with the Boy Scouts Association in Britain was retained. There were good reasons for this. All the Boy Scout Association handbooks, as well as badges and other equipment, were freely available to the Éire Scout Council, which also received an annual grant from the London scout headquarters. By retaining their link with London, Irish scouts thereby were guaranteed access to all world scout jamborees and world rover scout moots.

WORLD WAR II, 1939-45

Early in 1939 it was scouting as usual. Lord HolmPatrick reviewed the annual rally in Lord Iveagh's Gardens. It was the second last rally there; subsequently they were held at the Irish Rugby Union ground at Lansdowne Road. Twenty-four rover scouts attended the 3rd World Rover Scout Moot at Crieff, Perthshire, Scotland.

With the outbreak of war the Irish government declared its intention to remain neutral in the conflict. In a message to the B-P scouts the chief commissioner, Lord Powerscourt, wrote:

> War has been thrust upon the world again after the usual lapse of twenty years of so-called peace; and the flower of the manhood of many nations are now employed in tearing each other to pieces...
>
> Let us go about our business in normal fashion, keeping the home machinery greased and running as in times of peace, shouldering the load of others who have gone to higher service...
>
> We scouts are not soldiers, but we are a disciplined body and we are non-combatants; our duties lie on the home front and let us see that we do our bit...
>
> Our duty is to be loyal to our country and its government and to frustrate anything and everything that we may see which is damaging or calculated to damage its morale...

The scouts responded in characteristic fashion to the chief commissioner's message. With members of the Catholic Boy Scouts of Ireland (CBSI) and the Boys' Brigade, they provided volunteers for a Municipal Air Raid Protection Emergency Communications Service. They were among a large gathering of youth organisations in the Mansion House on 18 September to receive instruction on the use of gas-masks. Some helped in the staffing of the Blood Transfusion Service. Others were active in basic Air Raid Protection (ARP) activities. Over a hundred enlisted in the Irish and British forces and served at home and abroad. With their fellow-scouts in the CBSI they took part in the nationwide collection of waste paper and other such activities. The outbreak of the war in September 1939 saw the last edition of the quarterly *The Irish Scout,* which had been published from the beginning of 1937 and edited by G. S. Childs.

The B-P scouts in Northern Ireland were even more active during the war years. They acted as messengers between the armed services and civil defence posts. In addition, they were to be found helping in canteens, hospitals and supply depots. They assembled gas masks, assisted in the evacuation of children to safe country areas and collected waste paper and empty bottles. This last was to conserve the meagre supply of new glass.

DEATH OF B-P

Routine scouting activities continued at a reduced level. B-P died at his residence at Nyeri in Kenya on 8 January 1941 and memorial services were held eleven days later, on 19 January. Later on Irish scouts, north and south, supported a fund to build a house in London in memory of B-P after the war, a house where scouts from all over the world would find hospitality. In 1943 a thousand scouts at the annual rally at Lansdowne Road were reviewed by the new Chief Scout, Lord Somers, who complained that 'they marched badly'. This prompted a spirited response in the form of a sub-leader in the *Irish Times* of 26 June 1943. Lord Somers was reminded that B-P frequently drew attention to the fact that scouts were not 'toy soldiers' and recalled that when he inspected a troop and found that it specialised in tasty drilling performances he was not impressed. He confessed his preference that scouts should practise ambulance work, observation or useful handicrafts. The sub-leader concluded with a quote from B-P: 'Scouting has come to mean a system of training in citizenship, through games for boys and girls. It is complementary to the more scholastic training in schools.'

POST-WAR PERIOD

With the ending of the war some Dublin scouts undertook international relief work in Holland and Germany in 1945 and 1946 respectively. In 1945 Lord Rowallan was appointed Chief Scout of the British Commonwealth of Nations. During his first visit to Ireland the new chief inspected troops at

Dublin, Cork, Limerick, Drogheda and later in Northern Ireland. In his addresses he pointed to the world-wide character of their organisation and indicated that at that time five million scouts and three million guides were 'striving to keep the same law' throughout the world. He stressed that scouting was not merely a technique but a way of life and that duty to God was first in the promise of all scouts everywhere, concluding: 'Let us never forget that and let us strive our best to do our duty to Him, to thank Him for His goodness and to try and bring nearer the Kingdom to which we all hope in the end to attain'.

DEATH OF LORD AND LADY POWERSCOURT

Lady Powerscourt died in 1946 and her husband, Lord Powerscourt, died the following year, losses greatly felt by the Irish scout and guide movement. Both had been as much an inspiration to these movements in Ireland as B-P and Lady Baden-Powell had been on the world stage. In that year thirty-four Irish B-P scouts attended the 6th World Scout Jamboree at Moisson in France. An Ulster contingent led by Sir Christopher Musgrave, the Ulster Scout Commissioner, also attended it. The jamboree was organised by Scouts de France and its Chief Scout, General Lafont, presided at all major events. In sending his Apostolic Blessing to those attending the jamboree, Pius XII noted that they 'who had come together from so many different countries wished to give an example of understanding, of keenness and devotion which would not but inspire the world once more so grievously wounded by war'. In 1948, in the course of a message marking the 40th anniversary of the founding of the scout movement, Lord Rowallan noted that it then had four and a half million members in forty-one countries.

CHAPTER FOUR

Facing the Future

THE BOY SCOUTS OF IRELAND, 1949

I N 1949 the External Relations Act was repealed and the state was renamed the Republic of Ireland. Thereby the link with Britain and the British Commonwealth was severed. As it was legally impossible to continue as an integral part of the British Scout Association, the Éire Boy Scout Council set about ensuring that their organisation reflected these constitutional developments. Until then, while some voices had been raised at the grassroots on the need to meet nationalist sentiment, there was little enthusiasm for this at headquarters level. Thus in 1937 a suggestion was made to change the form of the scout promise and have a new member promise allegiance to the country and not to the king. This was rejected by the chief commissioner, the 8th Viscount Powerscourt, and imperial headquarters. In 1939 the issue was raised again, this time at a scoutmasters' conference but no change in the form of the promise was considered to be necessary. By 1941 many scout leaders wished to have the wording changed. However Lord Powerscourt again intervened and stated that the matter should not be submitted to the Éire Scout Council, that the country was still a part of the British Commonwealth of Nations and that a change would alienate the support of people who had helped to maintain the movement in the country.

Soon after the repeal of the External Relations Act the Éire Scout Council, with the approval of the Irish government, applied to the Boy Scouts International Bureau for recognition and to be registered as 'The Boy Scouts of Ireland'. At the 12th International Conference held in Norway the application was accepted with effect from 9 August 1949. In announcing the acceptance Colonel J. S. Wilson, director of the international bureau, stated: 'In making their application the Boy Scouts of Ireland expressed the hope that there would be no bar to the subsequent recognition of the Catholic Boy Scouts of Ireland'. The Boy Scouts of Ireland (BSI) next prepared a new handbook in which their rules were adapted to the new situation. In February 1952 this was published with the title *Policy, Organisation and Rules of the Boy Scouts of Ireland*. Not least among the changes made were those to the scout law, the promise and rules which had referred directly or indirectly to the British crown and imperial headquarters in London. To leave no doubt as to the national loyalty of Irish B-P scouts, the colour of the shirt was restricted to green and a green beret was introduced.

BOB-A-JOB WEEK, 1951

This feature of scouting began in 1914, when Sir Arthur Pearson, B-P's blind publisher, asked B-P if scouts could raise money for the blind. 'Not by begging or flag days,' replied B-P, 'but if there is any other way scouts would be willing to help'. Pearson suggested that money could be earned by doing odd jobs, whereupon scouts throughout Britain undertook a 'day of work' and in one week earned £32,000 for the fund for blind people. The idea was revived in Britain by F. Hayden Dimmock, editor of *The Scout*, in 1949 and taken up enthusiastically by the scouts in Northern Ireland. A Boy Scouts of Ireland bob-a-job scheme was launched in 1951; the week chosen was from 27 March to 2 April. Scouts throughout the country earned £839, £675 of which came from the Dublin city and county troops. The money was shared as follows: local troops: 30 per cent; local associations: 30 per cent; and Boy Scouts of Ireland executive, which bore the expenses of the scheme: 40 per cent. Subsequently the scheme became an integral part of the annual programme of most troops.

PRESIDENT SEÁN T. O'KELLY ATTENDS ANNUAL RALLY, 1952

Official appreciation for the manner in which the B-P scouts had repositioned themselves in the life of the country in 1949–50 was soon forthcoming. When in November 1951 Colonel J. S. Wilson, director of the World Scout Bureau, arrived for a two-week tour of scouting in the country he was received by the president at Áras an Uachtaráin and by the lord mayor at the Mansion House. Then in the following May President Seán T. O'Kelly took the salute at the march past and addressed more than 3,500 scouts, guides, rovers, rangers, cubs and brownies at Lansdowne Road. In his address he complimented them on their splendid turnout and emphasised the importance of self-control, self-discipline and physical exercise. He also exhorted them 'to remember at all times that we are Irish and Irish people with a distinct mentality, and belong to a country that has no mean past'. 'This country,' he continued 'down the centuries has done many noble things for the uplifting of the people both at home and all over the world'. However, Catholic membership, apart from the sea-scout groups, continued to be insignificant. (For the religious affiliation of the Dublin association groups in 1955, see Appendix 1.)

OTHER NOTABLE EVENTS AT HOME IN THE 1950S

In 1953 training courses were held for scout leaders in Powerscourt demesne. They were held again in 1954, with R. F. (John) Thurman, camp chief of Gilwell Park training centre, in attendance. In Northern Ireland courses were held at the training centre at Hillsborough, County Down. In 1955 Major General D.C. Spry, director of the World Scout Bureau, visited troops throughout the country, north and south. He reminded them that they belonged to a movement with a membership of six and a half million worldwide and stressed the importance of the 'daily good turn'.

In 1956 there was a successful annual rally of guides and scouts at Lansdowne Road and the Artane Boys Band made the first of its many appearances at this event. A new more commodious headquarters was formally opened at 66 Lower Leeson Street by General Richard Mulcahy, TD, minister for education, with Alderman Robert Briscoe, TD, lord mayor, in attendance. Also in 1956 Dermot A. James was appointed the association's public relations officer. An active member of the 33rd Dublin (Sandford) Scout Group since 1936, he had for some years been contributing the 'Scout notes' in the *Evening Mail* and later in the *Evening Herald*. In 1957, to mark the 50th anniversary of the scout movement, Dublin scouts organised a commemorative tree planting in Powerscourt demesne. In 1958 their annual rally was inspected by Jack Lynch, TD, minister for education. He was effusive in his praise of the guides and scouts and told them that the bearing, deportment and behaviour of the CBSI, who had recently visited Lourdes, had won the acclaim and esteem of people from many lands. In 1959 the remaining ties which linked the Irish B-P scouts with the (UK) Scout Association were severed.

NOTABLE EVENTS ABROAD IN 1950S

In 1951 nine Irish B-P scouts, five from Dublin and two each from Cork and Waterford, attended the 7th World Scout Jamboree at Bad Ischl in Austria, as did an Ulster troop led by Wilfred Brennen. In the following year Irish scouts were represented at the first world scout leaders indaba at Gilwell Park. 'Indaba', a South African word meaning 'a meeting of chiefs', was used to describe a gathering of scout leaders from all over the world. Its aim was to update them about developments in scouting. In 1953 twelve rover scouts participated in the 5th World Rover Moot at Kandersteg, Switzerland, and in 1954 a party of Dublin scouts were at the 5th Scottish International Jamborette at Blair Atholl.

In 1955 the 8th World Scout Jamboree was held in Canada at Niagara-on-the-Lake, two miles from the famous falls. Four Irish and thirty-seven Ulster scouts attended. Notwithstanding the determined efforts of the Canadian organisers to have the Irish contingent march under a banner which read 'Éire', which at that time was used by some British journalists as a belittling term, the Irish scouts insisted on having the alternative and more widely understood 'Ireland'. In 1957 a jamboree to mark the fiftieth anniversary of the Boy Scout Association, was held at Sutton Coldfield, near Birmingham. Much effort was put into preparing for the jubilee celebration and an Irish contingent of 465 attended, as well as five troops of Ulster scouts. One of the most memorable events of the jamboree was when Lady Baden-Powell led the assembled scouts in the scout promise, each speaking in his own language. By 1958 there were three Air Scout units in Belfast. In 1959 Patrol Leader Michael Webb was selected to attend, with Group Scoutmaster James McKee, the 9th World Scout Jamboree at Makiling near Manila in the Philippines which was also attended by three scouts from Northern Ireland.

FEDERATION OF IRISH SCOUT ASSOCIATIONS, 1965

By the beginning of the 1960s, there were thirty-one B-P scout groups in Dublin city and county and twelve elsewhere, with a membership of under 2,000. The monthly *Irish Scouting News* was published during the 1960s and into the 1970s. In 1960 the B-P scouts organised the 1st Irish International Scout Camp at Colonel H. T. W. Clements's Lough Rynn Estate, Mohill, County Leitrim. It was most successful and was featured on RTÉ. In 1963 and 1967 they were represented at the 10th and 11th World Scout jamborees at Marathon, near Athens, and in Idaho, USA, as were the scouts of Northern Ireland. In May 1964 they organised a conference of international scout commissioners at the Grand Hotel, Malahide, Dublin. But the most notable event in the 1960s and perhaps in the association's history was the establishment with the CBSI of the Federation of Irish Scout Associations (*Co-Chumann Gasóga na hÉireann*) (FISA) on 1 March 1965. This facilitated the international recognition of the CBSI together with the Irish B-P scouts by the World Organisation of the Scout Movement (WOSM). As the CBSI had most to gain from this new international arrangement, their members completed much of the preparatory work for this development. Eventually the proposal that the two scout associations should form a federation was approved at separate and joint meetings of the BSI and CBSI in 1964 and 1965. While both associations thereafter continued to run their own internal programmes, their aim was to combine more and more in joint ventures and to represent Ireland jointly at international events. In 1968, in order to adapt to the new structure the Boy Scouts of Ireland renamed itself the Scout Association of Ireland (SAI) and completed a series of major changes with regard to uniforms, badges, titles and organisation. Also in 1968 the new venture scout section, with a lower age-range than the rovers section which it replaced, was launched, as was a beaver scout section for younger children. In 1968 the Scout Association organised the 2nd Irish International Scout Camp in Westport, County Mayo.

1970S AND 1980S

In the 1970s there was a significant increase in the membership of the B-P scouts in the Republic, to just over 5,600. This increase in membership occurred mainly because large numbers of Catholics joined the SAI. In adapting to the rising demands on the time and the new interests of boys, there was less emphasis on hikes and camping. Weekend breaks to attend international rugby and soccer matches became a part of the programme of some troops.

As cooperation between the two associations increased, there was a desire on their part to link up with the Northern Ireland Scout Council (NISC). This was the new title of the authority administering the B-P scouts in Northern Ireland, following the restructuring of the Boy Scouts Association in the UK in 1967. In the mid-1970s the NISC had a membership of over 11,000. It also had a remarkable chief commissioner in Surgeon Wilfred Brennen. He had pioneered the beaver scout programme for six–eight-year-olds and, although a similar programme had been followed in Canada, he is credited with ensuring its adoption by B-P headquarters in London. The state of the association in Northern Ireland was a tribute to the resolute manner in which scouts refused to allow themselves, in spite of much provocation, to be deflected from their scouting in the 1960s, 1970s and early 1980s. During those traumatic years their headquarters were destroyed on more than one occasion. Irwin Scott of the 1st Dungannon was grievously injured in an attack on the Scott family business in 1977 and Bill McConnell, commissioner for Crawfordsburn, NISC's national camp site and training centre, near Belfast, was murdered in 1984.

Tripartite conferences of the CBSI, NISC and SAI were held during the 1970s, the first in Dublin, the second in Newcastle, County Down. In 1975 the FISA and Northern Ireland scouts were represented at the 13th World Scout Jamboree at Lillehammer in Norway. Full cooperation between the associations in the Republic had still to be achieved and the SAI took full responsibility for organising the 3rd Irish International Scout Camp at Woodstock demesne, Inistioge, County Kilkenny, in 1978. The attendance of 5,000 was more than double that of the two previous Irish international scout camps.

GIRLS JOIN A SCOUT TROOP

In 1980 girls joined a scout troop for the first time in the Republic of Ireland. It happened fortuitously. Father Denis Costello, Catholic chaplain to Sallynoggin Senior College, decided to form a troop in the college. He discovered that funds were available to this end. However, as the college was coeducational, these could not be used unless the troop was open to both girls and boys. This was not feasible at that time in the CBSI so he requested that the troop be affiliated to the SAI. A short time previously the leadership of the SAI, mainly owing to pressure from parents, had decided to open membership of the scouts to girls. Thus they had no objection to a troop with boys and girls and the Sallynoggin Senior College troop was registered, the first mixed troop in the country.

1980–2005

By the 1980s the SAI had about 6,000 members and by then a majority were Catholics. Apart from the Dublin area, there were troops or units in many places, including Arklow, Bray, Cavan, Cork (5), Drogheda, Dundalk, Enniskerry, Greystones, Letterkenny, Limerick (2), Raphoe, Sligo (2) and Waterford (2). In a number of these places troops were associated with Church of Ireland grammar schools.

In 1982 the NISC organised an international scout camp at Castle Archdale Country Park, Belleek, County Fermanagh.

Between 1980 and 2005 the two scout associations in the Republic worked ever more closely together. They jointly organised Irish international camps and jointly represented Ireland at world scout jamborees. The leadership of both associations also availed of every opportunity to develop further their links with the NISC. In 1985 its membership stood at more than 13,500 and to celebrate seventy-five years scouting in the province it published Margaret Bell's *A History of Scouting in Northern Ireland*. From 2000 onwards the SAI was an active participant in the intensive negotiations which led to the establishment of the new Scout Association, named Scouting Ireland (SI), for the new century.

Religious affiliation of Dublin Association Groups in 1955

1st	Dublin, Lord Holmpatrick's Own – Fairview	Catholic
3rd	Dublin, Stillorgan	Church of Ireland
5th	Dublin, 1st Port, sea scouts – Ringsend	Catholic
6th	Dublin, Leeson Park	Church of Ireland
7th	Dublin, Donnybrook	Church of Ireland
8th	Dublin, Clontarf	Methodist
10th	Dublin, Kiltiernan	Church of Ireland
11th	Dublin, Zion	Church of Ireland
12th	Dublin, 5th Port – Dollymount	Catholic
14th	Dublin, Mountjoy School	mainly Church of Ireland
15th	Dublin, Malahide	Church of Ireland
16th	Dublin, Jewish	Jewish
17th	Dublin, Blackrock	Church of Ireland
19th	Dublin, Glasnevin	Church of Ireland
20th	Dublin, Dundrum	Church of Ireland
21st	Dublin, 4th Port – Dodder	Catholic
22nd	Dublin, Sutton	Presbyterian
23rd	Dublin, Donore	Presbyterian

24th	Dublin, Pack-Beresford's Own – Leeson Street	Catholic
25th	Dublin, Mount Merrion	Church of Ireland
27th	Dublin, St Andrew's College	Presbyterian-Church of Ireland
30th	Dublin, Dún Laoghaire	Church of Ireland
31st	Dublin, Rathfarnham	Church of Ireland
32nd	Dublin, Rathgar	Presbyterian
33rd	Dublin, Sandford	Church of Ireland
34th	Dublin, Raheny	Church of Ireland
40th	Dublin, Clondalkin	Church of Ireland
41st	Dublin, Dalkey	Church of Ireland
42nd	Dublin, Killiney	Church of Ireland

Total groups 29: Church of Ireland 19; Presbyterian 3; Methodist 1; Jewish 1; Catholic 5

PART II

Fianna Éireann

Origins
The Early Years
Involvement in Easter Rising and War of Independence
The Struggle Continues
The Last Phase

CHAPTER ONE

Origins

IRISH REVIVAL

NA FIANNA ÉIREANN, generally known as Fianna Éireann (FÉ), was founded in 1909 against the background of the Irish Revival which occurred at the end of the nineteenth and the beginning of the twentieth centuries. The Gaelic Athletic Association (GAA) was set up in 1884 to foster Gaelic football, hurling, handball and rounders. The Irish Literary Society and the Irish Literary Theatre were established in 1892 and 1898 respectively to stimulate literature and playwriting which would be distinctively Irish, though written in English. Most importantly of all, the Gaelic League (Conradh na Gaeilge) was founded in 1893 to promote the Irish language, literature and culture. The Irish Cooperative Agricultural Society was formed in 1894 to direct and spread the cooperative movement. Inghinidhe na hÉireann (Daughters of Ireland), inaugurated in 1900, supported separatism, the Irish-Ireland movement and women's suffrage. Cumann na nGaedheal was founded in 1900 to promote Irish industry and as a coordinating body for smaller societies whose aim was to oppose English influence in Ireland. The Abbey Theatre opened its doors in 1904 as a centre for promoting the work of Irish playwrights. Sinn Féin was a political movement that evolved between 1905 and 1908. Arthur Griffith, the editor of the movement's paper Sinn Féin, stated 'Our declared object is to make England take one hand from Ireland's throat and the other out of Ireland's pocket.'

BADEN-POWELL SCOUTS – A CHALLENGE
The Baden-Powell (B-P) scouts presented a challenge to the Irish-Ireland community at large. An article in the *Irish Nation* of 19 June 1909 reflected on the possible social benefits which might accrue to the nation if a similar organisation were to be formed in Ireland. While acknowledging the phys-

ical benefits of the GAA, the author urged a nationalist version of this youth organisation which trains 'youths and men in habits of obedience and discipline and teaches them to honour and glory in the British empire'. The B-P scouts were seen as an even greater challenge by the promoters of the Irish Revival. In 1909 Baden-Powell had written to Patrick H. Pearse and, aware of his reputation as a headmaster and educationalist, invited him to set up an Irish branch of the boy scouts. Pearse refused the invitation, declining 'to make potential British soldiers out of Irish boys'. In her account in *Nodlaig na bhFiann 1909* Constance Countess Markievicz wrote:

> It was some time in March 1909 that I read an account in the *Irish Times* of 800 little Irish boys being paraded in brigades and sections before the lord lieutenant. Somehow the idea of these Irish lads haunted me...Nothing could be sadder than seeing these boys saluting the flag which flew in triumph over every defeat this nation has known ...The idea came to me of starting an organisation for boys, an organisation that would weld the youth of Ireland together to work and fight for Ireland.

IRISH REPUBLICAN BROTHERHOOD

Few were more opposed to a youth organisation which would produce loyal British subjects and British soldiers than members of the Irish Republican Brotherhood (IRB). Not surprisingly its members played a major role in the establishment and development of FÉ as an alternative to the B-P scout organisation. The IRB was founded in 1858 and organised a Rising in 1867 which failed not least because of bad planning and betrayal. In 1869 a supreme council was elected. Under a new constitution members were obliged to do their utmost to establish an independent Ireland, to be faithful to the supreme council and government of the Irish Republic and to obey their superior officers and the constitution of the IRB. The IRB exercised considerable influence through its policy of infiltrating nationalist organisations, from the founding of the GAA in 1884 onwards. In 1907 the unreconstructed Fenian, Thomas J. Clarke, who had spent fifteen years in prison following his arrest while on 'a dynamiting mission to England', returned to Dublin from New York. Inspired by him, members of the IRB rallied behind a more militant policy.

Prior to that time the IRB, a secret, oath-bound society, was content to remain behind the scenes and to continue to gain an increasing measure of influence and even control over the other organisations that were developing the new national consciousness. But members of the IRB were also ever on the lookout for an opportunity to establish a military organisation to exploit this new phenomenon. Countess Markievicz provided them with an ideal opportunity to this end when in June 1909 she established a youth movement, the 'Red Branch Knights', as an alternative to the B-P scouts. For the IRB, the chief merit of this new movement was that, as ostensibly a mere rival to the B-P scouts, it was less likely to attract the attention and active opposition of the British authorities and Irish constitutionalists.

CONSTANCE COUNTESS MARKIEVICZ AND THE BEGINNINGS OF FIANNA ÉIREANN

Constance Gore-Booth was born in 1868 and raised at her ancestral home at Lissadell House, Drumcliff, County Sligo. She studied art in London and Paris. In 1900 she married Kazimierz Markievicz and thereafter styled herself Countess Markievicz. She was attracted to Sinn Féin by reading the *United Irishman*, edited by Arthur Griffith. In 1906 she joined Inghinidhe na hÉireann and contributed to its monthly *Bean na hÉireann* from 1908 onwards. In 1908 she joined Sinn Féin. Until her death in 1927 she was a leading Republican and an implacable opponent of British rule in Ireland.

From March 1909 onwards she was determined to set up a nationalist boy scout movement. By that time she was an executive member of Sinn Féin and argued publicly and privately for such an initiative. She received little encouragement from Arthur Griffith and other Sinn Féin leaders. But Helena Moloney, a fellow-member of Inghinidhe na hÉireann, Bulmer Hobson, Dr Patrick MacCartan and Seán McGarry, all members of the IRB, joined her in an informal committee to organise the new youth movement. In June, on the recommendation of their teacher, John O'Neill, eight boys from the St Andrew's Christian Brothers national school at Westland Row became the first members of the organisation. With others they met at the residence of Countess Markievicz in Frankfort Avenue, Rathgar and engaged in drill and other exercises. She named the new organisation 'The Red Branch Knights' to linking it with the legends of Cuchulainn and the Ulster Cycle. In the meantime in *Bean na hÉireann* of July 1909 the Countess announced that a branch of the National Boy Scouts had been formed which the promoters hoped would be the nucleus of a national volunteer army. In the following issue of *Bean na hÉireann* one of the first members of the new organisation stated that the new boy scouts were to be recruits for the future army of Ireland and appealed to every Irish boy to join their ranks.

Little progress was made by the new scouts in the early months. From the outset they themselves decided to appoint their leaders and run the organisation. Yet not one of them was competent in drill, semaphore or any other scouting skill. Weekend hikes and a camp in the Dublin mountains near the Countess's cottage at Balally, Dundrum, proved to them how much they had to learn about scouting. Undeterred, the Countess hired a hall at 34 Lower Camden Street for the twice-weekly meetings.

FIRST MEETING OF FIANNA ÉIREANN

After a few months the Countess invited Bulmer Hobson to take an active role in the organisation of the new movement. He had set up a successful youth club, named Na Fianna Éireann, in West Belfast in 1902 to run a hurling league for boys and to provide them with classes in the Irish language and Irish history. At his suggestion she agreed to re-name the new organisation Na Fianna Éireann (FÉ). After an announcement in the Gaelic League publication, *An Claidheamh Soluis*, on 14 August 1909 the first meeting of FÉ was held two days later in the hall at Lower Camden Street. There was opposition to a proposal that Countess Markievicz be elected president. In the event, Bulmer Hobson was elected president; Countess Markievicz and Patrick Walsh vice-presidents; Joseph Robinson and J. Dundon honorary secretaries; and Pádraig Ó Riain honorary treasurer of the camping fund. Con Colbert, who was to be one of FÉ's most committed members, joined at that meeting. Two dozen boys attended and the first cadre, An Chéad *Sluagh*, was formed. Within months a preliminary constitution was drafted. In less than a year a basic handbook was prepared, mainly by Pádraig Ó Riain, and later an office was acquired at 12 D'Olier Street.

From the outset it was clear that FÉ was different from its UK and US counterparts. The constitution set out its objective as 'The re-establishment of the independence of Ireland' and this was to be achieved by 'The training of the boys of Ireland, mentally and physically, by teaching scouting and military exercises, Irish history and the Irish language'. The declaration administered to members read: 'I promise to work for the independence of Ireland, never to join England's armed forces and to obey my superior officers'. The military nature of the new organisation was unmistakeable. According to the constitution, if members did not obey their superior officers, they could be court-martialled. The military emphasis in FÉ was also reflected in an admonition to members not to become involved in party politics.

ORGANISATION

FÉ was stated to be a national organisation open to all Irish boys between twelve and sixteen years of age who endorsed its constitution and made the FÉ promise, no matter to what class or creed or party they or their fathers belonged. It was to have a president, two vice-presidents, an honorary secretary and an assistant secretary and an honorary treasurer. The organisation had as its basic unit a squad of six to eight boys under a squad leader. Two squads formed a section under a section leader and two or more sections a *sluagh* (a company, literally a large group or crowd), under a *sluagh* leader. The *sluagh* was generally named after an Irish patriot. A number of *sluaighte* in one district, which could be a county or a city, were grouped under one of the district councils (*Coistí Ceanntair*). The controlling authority was the central council (*Ardchoiste*) with its smaller executive committee. The overall governing body was the *Ardfheis* (Congress), representative of the central council, district councils and *sluaighte*, which met annually in Dublin. Members of district councils and the central council were either *sluagh* leaders or secretaries or treasurers who held no special rank. In 1913 the ranks of lieutenant, captain, commandant, adjutant and quartermaster were introduced and districts were renamed battalions. In a further reorganisation in 1915 a headquarters staff was formed with the ranks of chief of staff, adjutant-general, quartermaster-general and directors of training and organisation. The first offices of the headquarters' staff were in Findlater Place off O'Connell St. Initially the boys elected their own officers in the *sluaight*. However in 1918 this experiment in self-government was ended and thereafter all officers were appointed by general headquarters.

UNIFORM, FLAG, BADGES, RANKS

There were two recommended uniforms, both of which were to be of Irish manufacture. The first was 'a kilt uniform with a dark or olive green kilt and saffron cloak (*brat*) worn over a green jersey with cuffs and shoulder straps. The second was 'a knicks uniform' of olive-green shirt with two rows of brass buttons, and shoulder straps; and blue shorts or breeches. And with each uniform a dark-green felt sombrero was worn, together with a leather belt and black shoes and stockings. The FÉ flag was blue with a golden sunburst in the bottom right-hand corner and the title 'Na Fianna Éireann' in gold running across the field over the rays of the sunburst. The badge was a circular enamel brooch in green, white and gold with a golden sunburst and pike head in a green centre and the motto 'Cuimhnige ar

Luimneach agus ar fheall na Sasanagh' ('Remember Limerick and the treach-ery of the English') in the outer white circle. There were different rank badges for a Fianna, 3rd class, 2nd class and 1st class, and there were differ-ent cuffs and shoulder straps for squad leader (equivalent to an army cor-poral), section leader (equivalent to a sergeant) and *sluagh* leader (equivalent to a lieutenant or captain). In the early years long knives ('French bayonets') were worn on the belts.

CHAPTER TWO

The Early Years

EARLY DEVELOPMENT AND ACTIVITIES

IN SEPTEMBER 1909 classes in the Irish language and history were organised for *An Chéad Sluagh* and in October and November they had lectures from Countess Markievicz and Dr Patrick MacCartan. In November a second troop, formed in Drumcondra, was named *An Dara Sluagh*.

In 1910 the two Dublin *sluaighte* organised a concert during Easter week. In July three new Dublin *sluaighte* were formed in James Street, John Street and Sandwith Street respectively. On 1 August the Dublin *sluaighte* camped in the grounds of the residence of Countess Markievicz at Belcamp Park, Raheny, and on 7 August organised the first of their annual open-air concerts (*aeridheachts*) at Croydon Park, Fairview. On 21 August the first FÉ *Ardfheis* was held in the Mansion House, where they were to be convened annually until 1915. With Bulmer Hobson absent in Belfast, Countess Markievicz presided. 'The movement', she said, 'is doing excellent work in training the present generation of boys to be capable citizens of the Irish nation – strong in physique and mind, and infused with intense love of country.' She also expressed her hope that they would be 'pioneers of the national army of Ireland'. In his report Pádraig Ó Riain, who had become honorary secretary, stated that seven *sluaighte* had been affiliated, five in Dublin, one in Waterford and one in Glasgow and that the membership of each *sluagh* ranged from twenty to sixty. The following officers were elected: president: Countess Markievicz; vice-presidents: Bulmer Hobson and Councillor Gregan PLG; secretary: Pádraig Ó Riain; assistant secretary: Michael Lonergan; and treasurer: James Gregan.

In October members took part in processions lobbying for better support for the Irish language. They also organised local gaelic football and hurling leagues. In November new *sluaighte* were formed at Belfast,

Clonmel and Waterford and in December at Derry and Limerick. The *slu-agh* in Belfast was set up largely owing to the efforts of Annie O'Boyle. At that time also a *sluagh* was formed in Cork. It was established when Countess Markievicz visited the city for that purpose at the invitation of Tomás MacCurtain, who later, while was serving as lord mayor, was assassinated by members of the crown forces. For a brief period there were rival groups of 'Republican' scouts in Cork and Waterford. The most significant development at this time was the appearance of *Irish Freedom*, which was edited by Bulmer Hobson until June 1914. It carried reports on FÉ in practically all its monthly issues from November 1910 to December 1914, when it was suppressed by virtue of the Defence of the Realm Act.

In June 1911 *Irish Freedom* reported on the activities of six Dublin *sluaighte*. It also featured *sluaighte* from Belfast, one of which claimed to have over a hundred members with an ancillary *sluagh* of sixty girls. On 22 June George V was crowned king. Twenty thousand attended a meeting in Dublin to protest against his coronation as king of Ireland. Members of FÉ helped to distribute handbills for the meeting at which Dr Patrick MacCartan was one of the speakers.

On 7 July the king was formally received in Dublin. On that day 300 members of the Dublin Fianna joined the traditional Republican pilgrimage to the grave of Wolfe Tone at Bodenstown, near Sallins, County Kildare. The contingent included their pipers band. They led the procession to the graveyard and formed the guard of honour around the grave of the patriot during the customary oration. On the same day Countess Markievicz and other members of the Fianna attempted to make a public protest against the royal procession as it passed through College Green.

FÉ's second *Ardfheis* was held on 16 July 1911. A draft of the constitution was promulgated. It was reported that new *sluaighte* had been formed at Athlone, Dundalk, Limerick, Listowel, Maryboro (Portlaoise), Rathkeale and Waterford However, to instil a new urgency into efforts to establish the organisation throughout the country, the *Ardchoiste* was directed to meet every three months to this end. By year's end the number of *sluaighte* in Dublin and in Belfast had risen to seven. In October a branch of the Gaelic League for the Dublin Fianna was established and Patrick H. Pearse delivered an inspiring address to the Fianna at the inaugural meeting. Also in 1911 the supreme council of the IRB set up a circle, which they named the John Mitchel circle, for officers of FÉ, with Con Colbert as centre and Pádraig Ó Riain as secretary. In November Fianna *sluaighte* took part in the 'Manchester Martyrs' commemorations in different parts of the country.

LIAM MELLOWS

Liam Mellows was a central figure in the early years of FÉ. He was born on 25 May 1892 at Ashton-under-Lyne in Lancashire to a father serving in the British army, and was later raised by his grandparents at Inch, County Wexford. He was educated at the Cork, Portobello and the Royal Hibernian military schools. Influenced by *Irish Freedom* and Tom Clarke, he had joined FÉ in the autumn of 1911 and soon became secretary of the Dublin District Council. In addition he acted as leader of *sluaighte* at Inchicore ('Patrick Sarsfield') and Dolphin's Barn ('Brian Boru'). Subsequently he was sworn into the John Mitchel, that is the FÉ circle of the IRB, by Con Colbert.

The third *Ardfheis* was held on 14 July 1912. Representatives of *sluaighte* from the four provinces attended. Pádraig Ó Riain, the honorary secretary, announced that a guarantee fund was to be opened to enable the *Ardchoiste* to hire Liam Mellows as a full-time organiser. This was necessary as the resources available to FÉ and the *Ardchoiste* were always very limited. At the outset members were able to use Countess Markievicz's house and the hall she rented for their exercises, and there was a substantial donation from Sir Roger Casement. Subsequently there were affiliation fees from the *sluaighte* and from time to time funding was provided by the IRB, who were also active in recruiting members of FÉ. In a report submitted to the fourth *Ardfheis* on 13 July 1913 Mellows stated that since his appointment as organiser on 12 April 1913 he had visited existing *sluaighte* and formed new groups in Counties Wexford, Waterford, Carlow, Kilkenny, King's County (Offaly), Westport and Roscommon. In a series of articles on 'The Irish Boy Scouts' by 'An Irish Volunteer Officer' in the *Gaelic American* in April, May and June 1917 Mellows later recalled the hardship and difficulties he faced as an organiser of FÉ at that time. As he went around the country organising FÉ, he also swore young men into the IRB.

CONTINUING DEVELOPMENT AND EXPANDING ACTIVITIES

In the early months of 1912 *sluaighte* were formed at Cork, Donegal, Newry and Wexford. In the *Irish Freedom* of June the FÉ report included 'A manifesto to the boys of Ireland', as well as instructions on Morse code and signalling. Members distributed handbills advertising Feiseanna and Republican commemorations and became a familiar sight at Irish-Ireland gatherings. At football and hurling matches they sold copies of *Irish Freedom*, which by that time had a circulation of 6000. They also took part in a campaign to counter an enlistment drive by the British army.

At the *Ardfheis* on 14 July 1912 the constitution and rules were emended.

One change voted through was to open the membership to girls. This had been urged by the girls' *sluagh* in Belfast and was supported by Countess Markievicz. Within a month the *Ardchoiste* held a plebiscite of members on the issue and this change was rejected. From this time until 1922 the leaders of FÉ, nearly all of whom, apart from Countess Markievicz, were members of the John Mitchel Circle of the IRB, met before each *Ardfheis* to ensure it was run along 'proper lines'. Later, following the restructuring of the organisation in 1915, they ensured that, while each year, with the exception of 1917, Countess Markievicz was elected at the *Ardfheis* to be the titular head of FÉ, she did not have a seat on the *Ardchoiste* or serve on the organisation's GHQ.

By the end of 1912 there were about 1,000 members in twenty-two *sluaighte*, with district councils at Belfast, Cork and Dublin, and much effort was expended in improving the training of members and ensuring that they passed through the first, second and third class tests leading to the various grades of membership. FÉ was flourishing especially in Limerick. With the assistance of John Daly, the veteran Fenian, the local *sluagh* had built its own hall at Little Barrington Street, had a membership of 250 and a committed and able leader in Seán Heuston. As the movement grew and became more prominent in nationalist circles it attracted the attention of the authorities. The Dublin Metropolitan Police (DMP) began to keep its prominent members under surveillance and posted a member of the plain-clothes G-division outside the Dublin headquarters at Lower Camden Street.

A census taken on St Patrick's Day 1913 established that the membership of FÉ exceeded 1,000 countrywide. Membership in Cork city was forty. Thereafter this increased steadily: in 1914 it numbered fifty, in 1915 it was estimated at eighty and in 1916 at 100. The Dublin Fianna were engaged from 9 to 14 June 1913 in a summer fete at Croke Park to raise funds for St Enda's School (Scoil Eanna). Patrick H. Pearse had established the school initially at Cullenswood House in Ranelagh and transferred it in 1910 to a fifty-acre site at Rathfarnham. A *sluagh* of Fianna Éireann had been formed in the school in the autumn of 1910. It was called 'An Craobh Ruadh' ('The Red Branch') after the 'Red Branch Knights' of the Ulster cycle, the name that Countess Markievicz had originally chosen for the whole organization. At that time Con Colbert had joined the staff as a physical fitness instructor and took the *sluagh* for drill and signalling. He also swore some of the older boys into the IRB. Pearse, by virtue of his writing, lectures and orations at Republican gatherings, became an inspirational figure for members of FÉ. He also made the grounds of St Enda's available to the Dublin Fianna at all times for camping and other activities.

Over 200 members of the Dublin Fianna took part in the annual 'pilgrimage' to Bodenstown on 22 June. Thereafter attendance at this demonstration was to be an important event in the organisation's calendar. The fourth *Ardfheis* was held on 13 July. Further amendments were made to the constitution and the finalised draft was published in the *Irish Freedom* of September 1913. Those elected to the *Ardchoiste* were: president: Countess Markievicz; vice-presidents: Bulmer Hobson and Joseph Robinson; honorary secretary: Captain Pádraig Ó Riain; assistant secretary: Lieutenant Alfred White; treasurer: Lieutenant Frank Reynolds; organiser: Captain Liam Mellows; members: Captain Michael Lonergan (Dublin), Captain Con Colbert (Dublin), Lieutenant Seán Ó'Kelly (Belfast), Captain Seán Sinnott (Wexford), Edmund Leahy (Listowel) and Lieutenant Seán Heuston (Limerick). On 14 September the fourth annual FÉ *Aeridheacht* was held in Croydon Park, Fairview. In October new *sluaighte* were formed at Dundalk, Newry, Tuam and Tullamore. For many of the Fianna the highlight of 1913 was a lecture in their hall at Lower Camden Street by Major John MacBride. He was a life-long member of the IRB, had organised and led the Irish Brigade to fight against the British in the Boer war and was at that time a member of the Supreme Council of the IRB.

In 1913 a determined effort was made to promote the B-P scouts. In July, to this end, about 200 scouts from Manchester camped with the Dublin City scouts at Drimnagh, near Dublin. They were to be the forerunners of a number of other groups from Lancashire and Yorkshire.

Almost from the formation of FÉ its members of were involved in scuffles with B-P scouts. They regarded them as an adjunct of the British army. Some of the B-P troops were centred in military barracks, had military officers as leaders and access to the barracks' facilities. The older B-P scouts in these troops were called cadets and were eventually drafted into the Officers Training Corps.

The harassment of the B-P scouts intensified in July 1913. Members of the Dolphin's Barn *sluagh* attacked their camp at Drimnagh and some of the English and Irish scouts as they returned from hikes. The aim of the attackers, it seems, was to protest against and to 'confiscate' the Union Jack flying in the camp and carried on marches. As a result, the RIC had to mount a guard on the camp. The *Irish Times* of 1 August 1913 reported two of these incidents 'by young men who are believed to have an animus against the boy scout movement'. It also reported that the incident was discussed in the House of Commons.

Even when the Manchester scouts had returned home and plans for hundreds of other English scouts to succeed them had been shelved, the harassment of B-P scouts by members of FÉ continued. In the last week of August members of the Imperial Cadet Corps were occupying a cottage and its grounds at Kingston, near Dundrum. Con Colbert and about twenty other members of FÉ 'confiscated' the Union Jack and, as reported in the press, mounted a protest demonstration 'with French bayonets' against the wearing of British uniforms by the scouts. Colbert, who was regarded as the 'ringleader' by the authorities, was arrested and in the following October was bound to the peace for twelve months.

Members of FÉ also actively opposed the establishment of B-P troops. One such incident occurred at Ballybunion, County Kerry, in December 1913. The English employees at the Marconi wireless station advertised a public meeting to form a B-P troop. Edward Leahy and other members of the Listowel *sluagh* of FÉ attended and disrupted the meeting. Six weeks later a FÉ *sluagh* was formed in the seaside town.

From 1913 onwards the British army conducted an intensive recruitment campaign in Ireland. To counter this an anti-enlistment organisation was established. FÉ acted in conjunction with it by taking down recruitment posters, distributing anti-enlistment handbills and putting up anti-enlistment posters. And just as the British army attempted with bands parading to Irish patriotic tunes to drum up support for recruitment meetings FÉ used their pipers and fife bands to disrupt them.

In 1914 *sluaighte* were formed at Cashel, Clontarf, Gorey, Sandyford and elsewhere throughout the country. Nowhere was FÉ more active than in County Cork, where between 1914 and 1916 *sluaighte* were formed at Blackrock, Blarney, Clogheen, Cobh, Douglas, Mitchelstown, Riverstown and Youghal. In Cork city there were two *sluaighte*, one north of the River Lee, the other south of it. In June 1914 the Dublin *sluaighte* presented a military display at the fourth annual festival at St Enda's school. This included arms drill, skirmishing, semaphore signalling, first aid exercises and pioneering. Two weeks later this increasing military emphasis was evident at the annual Republican pilgrimage to Bodenstown. The senior members of the Dublin *sluaighte* marched on 19 June to Sallins, where they camped overnight and were joined by the junior members on the following day. Bodenstown 1914 was no longer a procession but a military demonstration with representatives from the Irish Volunteers, Irish Citizen Army, Cumann na mBan and FÉ, who formed the guard of honour around the grave of Wolfe Tone during the oration.

In September the *Fianna Handbook* was published. Much of it was prepared by Pádraig Ó Riain. There was an introduction by Countess Markievicz, an essay on Irish by *An Craoibhín Aoibhinn* (Douglas Hyde) in which he looked forward to the coming of an idyllic age, and reflections on chivalry by Sir Roger Casement. In 'The Fianna of Fionn' Patrick H. Pearse recalled the story of the Fianna and stated that they were the first heroic companionship to have borne that famous name; the Fenians of the nineteenth century were the second and FÉ the third. The handbook included a brief history of FÉ, the declaration made by each member, the various tests, the organisation's governing structures and how to form a *sluagh*. There were descriptions of the uniform, badges and flags, as well as paragraphs on FÉ's attitude to party politics and on the 'Spirit of Fianna Éireann'. The articles emphasised such traits as self-reliance, obedience, discipline, loyalty, trust and manliness. Members were never to do anything that would bring discredit upon Ireland or upon the Fianna. The handbook included the constitution and rules as amended at the *Ardfheis* in 1913. The major part consisted of chapters on drill, rifle exercises, camp life, knot-tying, signalling, first aid and swimming.

With the outbreak of World War I the recruiting campaign for the British army intensified as did the active opposition of FÉ to it. A Fianna Christmas annual, *Nodlaig na bhFiann*, edited by Percy Reynolds and Patsy O'Connor, appeared in December 1914. The financial success of the venture encouraged Reynolds and O'Connor to launch *Fianna* which was published monthly from February 1915 until Easter 1916. Initially intended as a monthly to convey the message of Irish nationalism to boys, it struggled unsuccessfully to compete with the weekly magazines for boys imported from Britain and was forced to widen its target audience to include adults.

CHAPTER THREE

Involvement in Easter Rising and War of Independence

DUBLIN LOCK-OUT, IRISH VOLUNTEERS, GUN-RUNNING AT HOWTH AND KILCOOLE, FUNERAL OF O'DONOVAN ROSSA

IN THE MEANTIME FÉ was becoming involved in national events. The Dublin Lock-Out in 1913 was the culmination of a protracted struggle between Dublin's organised labour, led by James Larkin, and the Dublin Employer's Federation directed by William Martin Murphy. By October tens of thousands of workers and their families were in dire straits. Countess Markievicz with the help of some friends set up a food kitchen in the basement of Liberty Hall. In this she was assisted by her 'Fianna boys', as she liked to refer to them.

Members of FÉ, such as apprentices and newspaper sellers, were themselves thrown out of work. They supported the demonstrations and protest meetings organised by Larkin and the other trade-union leaders. At a meeting in Sackville Street (now O'Connell Street) on 31 August, which Jim Larkin attempted to address, the Dublin Metropolitan Police baton-charged the crowd. Even though there was a warrant for his arrest, Countess Markievicz had sheltered him in her home, 'Surrey House' on Leinster Road, Rathmines. When accompanying Larkin to the meeting she was struck in the face by a policeman. On another occasion Patsy O'Connor, then an officer in FÉ, was struck on the head by a policeman, while providing first-aid to an injured worker during a baton charge. O'Connor died as a result of his injuries in July 1915.

Within months FÉ was involved in the establishment of the Irish Volunteers. In an article in *An Claidheamh Soluis* of 1 November 1913 Eoin MacNeill suggested that southern nationalists should form a volunteer movement on the lines of the Ulster Volunteer Force. Bulmer Hobson, with the help of the Dublin FÉ officers, organised a meeting to this end at the

Rotunda Rooms on 25 November. The meeting was stewarded by FÉ. Five of its members were elected to the Provisional Committee of the Irish Volunteers: Con Colbert, Michael Lonergan, Eamon Martin, Liam Mellows and Pádraig Ó Riain.

In September 1914 John Redmond urged the Volunteers to support Britain in the war. Of the nine members of the new Central Committee of the Volunteers who voted against this proposal three were FÉ members: Con Colbert, Eamon Martin and Liam Mellows. Bulmer Hobson, the fourth FÉ member, voted in favour of Redmond's proposal. From the autumn of 1913 FÉ officers were drilling members of the IRB in the National Foresters' Hall, Parnell Square. From the outset they helped with the training of the MacNeill-led Irish Volunteers and a number of these FÉ officers became officers in the new force. The crucial contribution made by FÉ to the Irish Volunteer movement was widely recognised. This was reflected in an address by Patrick H. Pearse in February 1914 when he stated: 'We believe that Fianna Éireann have kept the military spirit alive in Ireland during the last four years, and that, if the Fianna had not been founded in 1909, the Volunteers of 1913 would not have arisen'. Articles on FÉ appeared regularly in the Volunteers' newspaper, *The Irish Volunteer*, which was published from February 1914 until Easter 1916.

The next steps on the road to the Easter Rising of 1916 in which FÉ participated were the landing of arms for the Irish Volunteers at Howth on 26 July 1914 and at Kilcoole a week later. This landing of arms was organised by a committee which included Roger Casement, Erskine Childers, Darrell Figgis, Bulmer Hobson, Eoin MacNeill, The O'Rahilly and Mary Spring Rice. The arms were bought in Germany by Figgis and taken aboard Erskine Childers's yacht, the *Asgard*, for delivery to Howth.

The reception of the arms at Howth was supervised by Bulmer Hobson and other FÉ officers. On the morning of 26 July Liam Mellows and other members of FÉ, as well as some members of the Dublin Brigade of the Irish Volunteers, armed with revolvers, secured the harbour pier. Bulmer Hobson, who was in charge of the operation, was determined that no shots should be fired. But to ensure that the RIC from the local barracks were not able to interfere with the unloading of the arms, members of FÉ took a hand-drawn trek-cart full of oak batons to Howth with which to hold back the RIC from the harbour pier. That morning, led by the FÉ contingent, 800 Irish Volunteers set off on a routine march from Fairview. At Raheny, unaware of the imminent landing of arms, they were directed to continue to Howth. In the event the Irish Volunteers and the *Asgard* converged on the pier at Howth almost simultaneously. The handful of local police were successfully obstructed from protecting the pier by a cordon of FÉ members and Irish Volunteers, armed with the oak batons, and the landing of 900 rifles and ammunition was completed. FÉ members were again to the fore when the Volunteers with their arms were blocked at Clontarf on their way back to Dublin by a cordon of police and military. After a conversation between Bulmer Hobson and Assistant Police Commissioner William Harrell ended, the police and military moved forward. There followed a prolonged scuffle between them and mainly FÉ members. The latter did not concede their ground and even captured five rifles from the soldiers. This also enabled a cordon of Irish Volunteers to be formed behind which the landed arms were spirited away to safety. The FÉ trek-cart was also used to take away some of the rifles with the ammunition.

Six days later there was a second landing of arms at Kilcoole, County Wicklow. A cargo of six hundred rifles and ammunition was brought ashore. The landing was jointly planned and supervised by FÉ and the Irish Volunteers and of the fifty-one individuals selected to carry it out eleven were members of FÉ.

Members of FÉ were again prominent at the funeral of Jeremiah O'Donovan Rossa. A native of Ross Carbery, County Cork, he had been a life-long opponent of British rule in Ireland. He became a Fenian legend in his own life-time for his unbroken spirit in the face of extraordinary hardship during many years in prison. He died in New York and his body was brought home for burial in Ireland. Republicans transformed his funeral on 1 August 1915 into a great political demonstration. All the Irish-Ireland and republican organisations, including FÉ, took part in the funeral procession from the City Hall in Dublin, where his body had been lying in state, to Glasnevin cemetery. Members of the Fianna formed part of the guard of honour around the grave. There they heard Patrick Pearse's oft-quoted peroration:

> Life springs from death; and from the graves of patriot men and women spring living nations. The Defenders of this Realm …think that they have pacified Ireland …but the fools, the fools, the fools! they have left us our Fenian dead, and while, Ireland holds these graves, Ireland unfree shall never be at peace.

From this time onwards FÉ was the subject of close police surveillance. The fifth *Ardfheis*, which had to be postponed, was held in the Mansion House on 11 October 1914. Beginning in January 1915 a major restructuring of the organisation was undertaken. This was to align it with the Irish Volunteers and to cope with large numbers of new members. *Sluaighte* were no longer organised under district councils but into brigades and battalion formations. In training there was a clear change in emphasis from scouting to military exercises. These changes were presented at a convention of the *sluaighte* of Munster at Limerick in May and were approved by the sixth *Ardfheis* on 11 June 1915 held at 12 D'Olier Street. The *Ardchoiste* elected at the *Ardfheis* met on 24 July and appointed the following headquarters staff: chief of the Fianna (*Ard Taoiseach*): Pádraig Ó Riain; chief of staff: Bulmer Hobson; adjutant general: A.P. Reynolds; director of training: Seán Mac Aodha (Seán Heuston); director of organisation and recruiting: Eamon Martin; director of equipment: Leo Henderson; assistant director of equipment: Garry Holohan; director of finance: Barney Mellows. In August the Dublin Fianna were organised into the following battalion of nine companies: No. 1 (Camden Street), No 2 (Dolphin's Barn), No 3 (Inchicore), No 4 (Ranelagh), No 5 (Merchants' Quay), No 6 (North Frederick Street), No 7 (Blackhall Street), No 8 (Fairview), No 9 (Dollymount). Their respective Commanders were: P. Cassidy, Barney Mellows, Ernie Murray, Garry Holohan, Seán Heuston, Seán McLoughlin, Leo Henderson and Pádraig Ó Dálaigh. Michael Collender who was in charge of the battalion's band was killed later in 1915, while serving in France.

EASTER RISING 1916 AND THEREAFTER; WAR OF INDEPENDENCE

The Rising of Easter 1916 was planned by the military council of the IRB in the previous January. Eoin MacNeill, chief of staff of the Irish Volunteers, was not informed of the plan. On hearing of it, he confronted Patrick H. Pearse and Seán Mac Diarmada, who attempted to convince him that it would succeed. He was not persuaded and countermanded Pearse's order for the full mobilisation of the Irish Volunteers on Easter Sunday, which was crucial to the success of the uprising. Nevertheless Pearse, the other members of the military council and James Connolly decided to press ahead with the uprising on Easter Monday.

In the spring of 1916 FÉ officers, who were members of the IRB, were aware that a Rising was being planned. Others were not and some *sluaighte* spent the Easter weekend hiking in the Dublin mountains. Those who were informed of the imminence of the Rising in preparation for it set up the 'Fianna commando'. This was composed of officers and selected senior members of the Dublin *sluaighte*. In the overall plan this was to mobilise at

Skipper's Alley Hall, behind the church of Adam and Eve at Merchants' Quay, on Easter Sunday. It was to fight as a distinct unit and a detachment of it, under Paddy Daly, with Garry Holohan as his second in command, was detailed to capture and destroy the magazine fort in the Phoenix Park.

In the confusion following MacNeill's countermanding order the Fianna commando did not mobilise. On Easter Monday many members of FÉ, on receiving news of the outbreak of hostilities, reported to the nearest post held by Irish Volunteers. Paddy Daly, a carpenter, who had worked in the magazine fort, had informed the IRB and central committee of the Irish Volunteers about its layout and helped to prepare the plan to capture and destroy it. He mobilised the twenty-strong detachment of the commando which had been detailed to attack the magazine fort. They went to the Phoenix Park, pretending to be a football team. Some of them, idly kicking the ball, moved close to the sentry on duty. He was overpowered, as were the fifteen other soldiers at the Fort. The 'commando' set fire to the fort, the total destruction of which was averted only by the rapid arrival of troops from the nearby Islandbridge barracks. One of the soldiers guarding the fort was fatally wounded, as was the son of a member of the garrison as he cycled to the Islandbridge barracks to raise the alarm.

The Fianna commando was subsequently involved in an attack on Broadstone Railway Station, the capture of Linen Hall Barracks and fierce fighting in the North King Street area. Former FÉ officers were prominent at important outposts in Dublin during Easter week. Seán Heuston was in charge at the Mendicity Institute on Usher's Island; Con Colbert was in command at Watkins Brewery on Ardee Street and later at Marrowbone Lane Distillery; and Countess Markievicz was second in command at St Stephen's Green and the College of Surgeons. Liam Mellows, the former FÉ organiser, had command of the Irish Volunteers in Connacht. After the collapse of the Rising he went 'on the run;' and eventually made his way to the US.

Individual members of FÉ were to be found at practically all the Volunteer outposts, acting as scouts, dispatch carriers, cooks, and riflemen. Seven members of FÉ were killed in action, six in Dublin, one in Galway. Con Colbert and Seán Heuston were executed in Kilmainham Jail on 8 May. A number were wounded, among them Eamon Martin of the headquarters staff. Following the surrender most of the Fianna boys returned home. Those who were caught in the subsequent round-up by the military were held for a week in Richmond Barracks. On their release, they 'fell in' and defiantly marched away.

In the country at large FÉ, like the Irish Volunteers, did not take part in the Rising, owing to MacNeill's countermanding order. Thus, as was their practice, the FÉ in Cork city joined the local Volunteers on their parade on Easter Sunday. When they reached Macroom an order was given to dismiss and they returned home.

Less than a month after the Rising a meeting of Fianna officers who had participated in it and were at liberty, was held in the hall at Lower Camden Street. It was called to set up a committee to control the organisation in Dublin until the senior officers, who had been interned, were released. The following were appointed to this committee: 'The Provisional Committee of Control': chairman: Eamon Martin (then in the US); and Séamus Punch, Liam Staines, Theo Fitzgerald and Joseph Reynolds. In January 1917, after the general release of the prisoners from Frongoch and elsewhere during Christmas week, the headquarters staff was reconstituted as follows: chief of the Fianna: Countess Markievicz; chief of staff: Eamon Martin; adjutant-general: Barney Mellows; assistant adjutant general: P.J. Stephenson; quartermaster general: Garry Holohan; assistant quartermaster general: Alfred White; director of training and acting chief of staff: Seán McLoughlin. From April onwards, in breach of an order outlawing marching and drilling, the Fianna paraded openly through Dublin in uniform, often carrying hurleys. Their aim was to bolster nationalist morale after the debâcle of Easter week. They were involved in clashes with the Dublin Metropolitan Police, who attempted to block and break up these parades. The most serious clash was an attack on Inspector John Mills when he was arresting Count George Plunkett, who some months earlier had won the North Roscommon by-election for Sinn Féin. The attack occurred near Store Street on 10 July 1917. The inspector was struck on the head with a stick and died from his injuries two days later.

The new headquarters staff concentrated on an intensive recruiting campaign. Numerous *sluaighte* were formed throughout the country. In Dublin *sluaighte* were organised into two battalions: one north of the Liffey, the other south of it. In Cork similarly, the *sluaighte* were organised into groupings north of the Lee and south of it. The eighth *Ardfheis* was held in August at 41 York Street. On a motion, proposed by Countess Markievicz, Commandant Eamonn de Valera was elected Chief of the Fianna.

Thomas Ashe died on 25 September 1917, as a result of force-feeding while on hunger strike. There was a rising tide of public anger over the circumstances surrounding his death. Over 30,000 people including Archbishop William Joseph Walsh of Dublin, attended his funeral.

Reminiscent of the O'Donovan Rossa funeral, it was transformed by republicans into a huge political demonstration. The Fianna were prominent in the procession to Glasnevin. Subsequently such was the increase in recruitment to the organisation that it was estimated to have had at this time 20,000 members countrywide. The increase in membership in Tralee at that time was typical. The original *sluagh* was divided into three sections, each corresponding with the areas associated with the Irish Volunteer units and GAA clubs in the town. Boherbee had 109 members, Strand Road mustered 120 and Rock Street also had 120.

The British government attempted to impose conscription on Ireland in April 1918. It was opposed by nationalists of all degrees of intensity, including the Fianna commando which had been reorganised for this purpose. The subsequent successful anti-conscription campaign encouraged further recruitment to the Irish Volunteers and FÉ. At that time Seán MacBride, son of executed leader John MacBride, joined FÉ and attended meetings of his *sluagh* in the hall at Skipper's Alley. The meetings included drill and lectures on Irish history. He recalled Countess Markievicz, also Barney Mellows, then commander of the Dublin brigade of FÉ, coming on a number of occasions to speak to them. The activity MacBride enjoyed most was the *sluagh*'s weekend camps in the Dublin mountains.

The ninth *Ardfheis* was held in August at St Enda's School. Countess Markievicz was elected Chief of The Fianna, a position she was to hold until 1922. In October a group of the Dublin Fianna successfully defended the Sinn Féin office at 6 Harcourt Street when it was attacked by a mob of off-duty British soldiers and students from Trinity College. Notwithstanding the directive in the *Handbook* to members not to become involved in party politics, the Fianna were active in ensuring the landslide victory of Sinn Féin at the polls in the general election in December 1918.

The ambush of an RIC party at Soloheadbeg, County Tipperary, on 21 January 1919 marked the beginning of the War of Independence. On the same day Sinn Féin members returned in the general election of December 1918 constituted themselves the First Dáil Éireann. As the year progressed the number of attacks on crown property and ambushes on squads of police and soldiers increased. In August the Irish Volunteers took an oath of allegiance to Dáil Éireann and were subsequently called the Irish Republican Army (IRA). Earlier that year, at their tenth *Ardfheis* held in the Mansion House, FÉ had pledged their allegiance and had changed the pledge taken by members to:

1. A scout patrol in Londonderry at army headquarters, 1908. Patrol leader, Corporal Fred Baker, is second from the left in the front

2. Patrol leaders of 1st Hollywood with their scoutmaster, Robert Patterson, *c.* 1913

3. (Above) Group at second meeting of 33rd Dublin (Sanford), 1918. *Front row, left to right*: Willy Murphy, Jack Skelton, Frank Stearn and H. Pyper. *Back row, left to right*: unidentified, Jack McGinlay, Eric O'Brien and Rev Paul Quigley, founder of the 33rd

4. Lord Baden-Powell with Lord Powerscourt at Powerscourt demesne, 1928

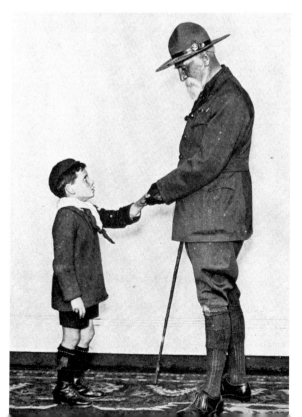

5. On the left is the Irish contingent marching as an integral part of the United Kingdom at the 1st World Scout Jamboree in London in 1920. At subsequent Jamborees, commencing with the 2nd held in 1924, Irish scouts marched behind the tricolour.

On the left is the earl of Meath, the oldest scout (he was then aged 80), with the youngest cub of the 1920 Jamboree

6. The Dublin Association's annual rally and sports at Lord Iveagh's grounds, St Stephen's Green, 1929. General William Creagh Hickie takes the salute and Fred Willis leads the 33rd Dublin in the march past

7. Chief Scout and Chief Guide, Lady Olave Baden-Powell, at scout and guide rally, Balmoral Showgrounds, Belfast, 1929

8. Irish scouts at 3rd World Scout Jamboree, in Arrowe Park, near Birkenhead, 1929. *Left to right*: V. Penney, H. Armstrong, J. Skelton, Plev Ellis, T. Hosgood and D. Adcock

9. Chief Scout, Lord Somers, officially opens the 'Wigwam' in the Powerscourt demesne, 1943. *Front row, left to right*: Percy Scott, camp warden, and Plev Ellis, scoutmaster, 33rd Dublin. *Back row, left to right*: A.W. Hurll, general secretary of Boy Scouts Association, London, Lord Powerscourt, Lord Somers, Miss Olive Armstrong, assistant chief commissioner cubs, and W.N. Carte, assistant chief commissioner training

10. The contingent selected to represent Northern Ireland at the 6th World Scout Jamboree in 1947 meeting the prime minister and the chief commissioner before setting out. *Front, left to right*: Sir Basil Brooke and Sir Christopher Musgrave

11. Irish scouts from Cork, Dublin and Waterford at 7th World Scout Jamboree at Bad Ischl, near Salzburg, in 1951. *Front row, left to right*: Billy Hamilton, 33rd Dublin, unidentified. *Second row, left to right*: Alan Harris, 2nd Waterford, Freddie Kerr, 32nd Dublin, Dermot James, 33rd Dublin. *Back row, left to right*: Tom Robinson, 2nd Waterford, unidentified, unidentified, unidentified. The camp gateway was designed by the bishop of Cashel and Ossory

12. Opening ceremony at 9th World Scout Jamboree at Makilin, near Manila, in 1959. Patrol Leader Michael Webb of 15th Dublin carries the Irish flag

---

13. Before setting out for the 10th World Scout Jamboree at Marathon in Greece in 1963 the Northern Ireland contingent present Irish dancing at Belfast Castle

14. (Above) Convocation at Balmoral, Belfast, 1974. *Front, left to right*: Wilfred Brennen, chief commissioner, Brian Fairgreaves, county commissioner, Stirlingshire, Scotland, and David Harrrison, Belfast county commissioner

15. At the international scout camp: 'Lakeland 1982' at Castle Archdale, County Fermanagh. *Left to right*: R.J. Clifford Boyd, assistant chief commissioner, Maj-Gen Michael J. Walsh, Chief Scout, David Harrison, chief commissioner, and Robert J. Brown, assistant chief commissioner

> I ...pledge my allegiance to the Irish Republic, and I promise to do all to protect her from all enemies, whether foreign or domestic. I also promise to obey my superior officers and to practise the code of honour.

From 1919 until the signing of the truce in 1921 individual members of FÉ, then declared to be an illegal organisation, provided intelligence and scouting for IRA units. Fianna active service units operated in Belfast and Cork, the one in Cork was composed of members of the *sluagh* centred in Blackpool. The Fianna were involved in acts of sabotage, raiding for arms and hundreds of them became IRA activists. They carried dispatches for IRA units throughout the country. But perhaps the most important role of FÉ members at that time was acting as couriers in Dublin, where they helped to link up Dáil Éireann with its various ministries and enabled Sinn Féin leaders to meet representatives of the press and distinguished visitors who were attempting to facilitate an end to hostilities. All these FÉ members belonged to the IRB circle, of which at that time Garry Holohan was the 'Centre' or chairman.

In Dublin the Fianna frequently raided for arms. In the late autumn of 1920 IRA and FÉ groups raided the same area at the same time on a number of occasions. There was a meeting of representatives of the IRA and FÉ GHQ staffs to deal with this overlapping and confusion. This produced what was called the 'army agreement'. In February 1921 it was communicated to the FÉ membership in 'Memorandum No 1, Fianna Éireann, GHQ, Dublin 1921'. (See Appendix 1.) Under the agreement FÉ was recognised as an integral corps of the republican army and details were given on the chain of command in this new relationship between the FÉ and the IRA. There were sections in the memorandum on training, operations, reports and communications. Paragraph 5 made clear what IRA GHQ regarded as the primary mission of FÉ:

> On attaining the age of eighteen a boy, unless his services are necessary for the successful management of the company, will be transferred to the Irish Volunteers...These transfers which are of the greatest importance must be made regularly and a record must be kept in each company of such transfers.

To implement the 'army agreement' a council was set up comprising three FÉ GHQ officers: Eamon Martin, Barney Mellows and Garry Holohan; and three Irish Volunteer GHQ officers: Dermot Hegarty, Gearóid O'Sullivan and Bob Price. The meetings of this council were presided over by a nominee of Cathal Brugha, the Dáil's minister of defence. As a result of the agreement, FÉ received a monthly grant from the department of defence from which the FÉ adjutant general, Barney Mellows, who had given up his civil employment, was paid a salary. The council supervised the reorganisation of the Dublin brigade of FÉ into five battalion areas corresponding to those of the IRA

The War of Independence ended with the truce between the crown forces and the IRA which took effect on 11 July 1921. During the hostilities, many members of FÉ were interned, including Countess Markievicz, who was in jail from May to October 1919 and September 1920 until July 1921. Four members were killed, one six weeks after the truce. At the twelfth *Ardfheis* soon after the truce Eamon Martin, director of organisation, reported that FÉ had 25,000 members throughout the country. However, Garry Holohan, chief of staff, in responding to this cautioned that this was only an 'on paper' figure and that half or two-thirds of that figure would be a more accurate estimate. The truce enabled Eamon Martin to organise an All-Ireland training camp at Artane in Dublin from 18–24 September 1921 and about that time also training camps were run by the five Dublin battalions. The emphasis in the training at the camps was on the use of arms. Following the truce the IRA, FÉ, Cumann na mBan and other national bodies in a show of strength took part in a parade at Smithfield in Dublin. FÉ units from all over Ireland were represented in the parade, which included 2,100 members of the Dublin brigade under the command of Garry Holohan. In the period between the truce and the outbreak of the Civil War hundreds of members of FÉ acted as republican police in support of the republican courts which had been established by Dáil Éireann.

CHAPTER FOUR

The Struggle Continues

THE CIVIL WAR

THE ANGLO-IRISH TREATY was signed on 6 December 1921. From the outset there was determined and widespread opposition to it, led by President de Valera and two of his cabinet colleagues, Cathal Brugha and Austin Stack. During the following months those who supported the treaty and those who opposed it did their utmost to gain control of Sinn Féin, the IRA, the IRB and FÉ. Sinn Féin, the IRA and the IRB split on the issue. FÉ did not.

Less than a week after the signing of the treaty the Supreme Council of the IRB met and voted eleven to four to support the treaty. The FÉ circle of the IRB, which was composed of most of the senior officers of FÉ, met in January. As was customary at meetings of IRB circles, a 'visitor' from another circle attended and was invited to act as chairman. The 'visitor' brought with him the Supreme Council's recommendation on the treaty. This was rejected, the 'visitor' was expelled and the circle dissolved itself.

The FÉ leadership moved quickly to ensure that the organisation remained unified and on the side of the anti-Treatyites. On 10 January 1922 Barney Mellows, adjutant-general, issued a circular to all *sluaighte* that political discussions were to be avoided and stating that future policy would be decided at the upcoming *Ardfheis*. This was subsequently fixed for 12 March. Perhaps because they anticipated opposition to the alignment of the organisation with the anti-Treatyites the FÉ leadership cancelled the *Ardfheis* on 28 February. In its place Barney Mellows, adjutant-general, organised a Munster convention of FÉ leaders in Cork on 17 March. In Munster opposition to the treaty was stronger than elsewhere and by this move the FÉ leadership no doubt hoped to get a ringing endorsement of their anti-treatyite policy.

The postponed thirteenth *Ardfheis* was held in the Mansion House on

16 April 1922. Barney Mellows presided. The *Ardfheis* pledged its allegiance to the Republic, in effect, the anti-treatyite cause. In the meantime two parades before prominent anti-Treatyites organised by the Dublin brigade of FÉ indicated where their loyalty lay. The first was a parade at St Enda's school which was inspected by Commandant Liam Mellows and Commandant Rory O'Connor. At the second in Croke Park the salute was taken by President de Valera and General Oscar Traynor. At these parades the general order of the day was: 'Report back to your units'. This was subsequently communicated to all members of FÉ and was especially directed to those who had decided to remain neutral on the issue of the treaty or those who had joined the pro-treaty national army recruited by the Provisional government.

Leo Henderson, a prominent member of FÉ prior to 1916, was involved in the incident which triggered the outbreak of the Civil War. He was one of the officers in the section of the anti-treatyite IRA who on 13 April 1922 took over the Four Courts and made it the republican military headquarters. While leading a raiding party on 26 June, he was arrested by a unit of the new national army. In retaliation his colleagues in the Four Courts kidnapped Lieut-General J. J. (Ginger) O'Connell, the army's deputy chief of staff. After a tense stand-off the army began shelling the Four Courts on the following day.

The first major consequence of this action was to ensure unity among the leaders of the anti-treaty IRA. The Dublin brigade, which was mainly anti-treaty, under its OC, Oscar Traynor, rallied to the support of their comrades in the Four Courts. They had already occupied a number of positions in the city centre, with headquarters in the Gresham-Hammam block of buildings on the east side of O'Connell Street. About 400 members of the Dublin brigade of FÉ had taken part in this action. They were present in considerable numbers in Barry's Hotel and the Hammam Hotel. FÉ had also placed a permanent guard on 38 North Great George's Street, which they used as their headquarters. Members of FÉ were in the small group which on 2 July made a final stand in the Hammam Hotel, during which Cathal Brugha was fatally wounded.

With Dublin secure the army of the Provisional Government turned its attention to the rest of the country. Many police and military barracks, evacuated by the crown forces, were occupied by units of the anti-treaty IRA who were helped by FÉ to garrison them. The army slowly cleared the anti-Treatyites from those positions and proceeded to gain control of the territory of the new Irish Free State. The anti-Treatyites attempted to defend a line from Limerick to Waterford. This led to serious clashes between the pro- and anti-Treatyites at Dungarvan, Kilmallock, Limerick, Passage West and Waterford. The Cork and Limerick *sluaighte* of FÉ were involved in these. FÉ was active in other areas also. In the period between the signing of the Anglo-Irish Treaty on 6 December 1921 and the end of the Civil War on 24 May 1923, sixteen members of FÉ were killed, many were wounded and hundreds were interned. Earlier on 8 December 1922 Liam Mellows and Joe McKelvey, who had been commandant of the Belfast battalion of FÉ, were executed. They had been in Mountjoy jail since the capture of the Four Courts and their execution was carried out in accordance with a reprisal policy adopted by the Provisional Government.

Nearly all members of FÉ who supported the Anglo-Irish Treaty went straight into the National Army. For the most part they had been officers in FÉ and they made up much of the command structure of the new force. Some were also active in the field. None more so than Paddy Daly. Veteran of the attack on the Magazine Fort and the fighting in North King Street during Easter week 1916, he went on to join the Dublin brigade of Irish Volunteers (later IRA). During the Anglo-Irish war he led the Active Service Unit of IRA GHQ, also known as 'Mick Collins's squad'. On joining the National Army he was placed in charge of the Dublin Guards, its most effective corps. They were given the responsibility of pacifying Kerry and rounding-up the active anti-Treatyites there. Towards the end of the campaign troops under his command matched atrocities with the anti-Treatyites and as a result his reputation was grievously damaged.

After their defeat in the Civil War the anti-Treatyites reorganised and styled themselves 'Republicans'. They regarded their former comrades who supported the Anglo-Irish Treaty and the Irish Free State that was established as a result of the treaty as 'Free Staters'. In the general election on 27 August 1923 Cumann na nGaedheal, the government party and the party of the pro-treatyites, had 63 candidates elected; the republicans/Sinn Féin, the party of the anti-Treatyites, 44; Labour 12; Farmers Party 15; and Independents 17. While the election results demonstrated the continuity of Republican support which had been obscured by the unpopularity of the Civil War, they also legitimised the Irish Free State's existence in terms of its constitutional basis and its claim to represent majority opinion in the twenty-six counties.

In May 1923, at the end of the Civil War, the anti-treatyite IRA dumped their arms. With military resistance no longer an option they subsequently rallied behind 'Sinn Féin Reorganised', which was established to continue the struggle for the 'Republic' by political means. With very few exceptions FÉ *sluaighte* no longer existed after the end of the Civil War. But with the assistance of a small group of members who had opposed the treaty, Countess Markievicz reorganised it in 1924. A new abbreviated *Handbook* was issued and the organisation's monthly *Fianna* reappeared. In deference to a prevailing public mood of rejection of armed conflict, the reorganised FÉ set out its aim as 'the training of the youth of Ireland to be honourable and self-reliant citizens'. It also proposed to 'safeguard national ideals throughout the land'. In accordance with this new policy the emphasis was to be on education and physical training, no longer on practising the use of firearms. Although for the most part a creation of the IRB prior to 1922, from the outset FÉ regarded itself as 'the national boy scouts of Ireland'. After 1922 it became, in effect, the boy scouts of the IRA and was known as the 'Republican Boy Scouts'.

Notwithstanding the statements of the reorganised FÉ implying a commitment to non-violent activities only, in 1925 other former members established a youth movement to work for the establishment of the 'republic' by peaceful means. Named Clanna Fodhla: The Irish Catholic Boy Scouts, it did not survive beyond a few years. The authorities in Northern Ireland and the Irish Free State were even less impressed by the new face of FÉ. From its establishment in June 1921 the administration in Northern Ireland declared FÉ to be an illegal organisation and its members were subjected to close surveillance and occasional harassment by the Royal Ulster Constabulary (RUC). In the Irish Free State from 1925 onwards its activities were disrupted under the Treasonable Offences Act and eventually it was also banned from 1931 to 1932. However the organisation survived, nowhere better than in Cork city where from the late 1920s until the mid-1930s membership stood at 300 and the local *sluagh* frequently held route marches and parades.

On the death of Countess Markievicz in 1927, George Plunkett succeeded as Chief Scout of FÉ. He was the second son of Count George Plunkett and had fought in the GPO alongside his brothers, Jack and Joseph Mary, during Easter week 1916. Released from prison in June 1917, he took part in the War of Independence. He opposed the Anglo-Irish Treaty and was arrested after the surrender of the Four Courts garrison on 30 June 1922. Released from prison in December 1923, he helped Countess Markievicz reorganise FÉ in 1924. He was a diligent Chief Scout. On a few occasions he even succeeded in gaining access to the senior classes of secondary schools to recruit for FÉ. Apart from a few brief interludes, he continued as Chief Scout until his arrest in May 1940 as part of the round-up of republicans at the start of the Emergency. Soon after his release, a few months later, he was killed in a road accident in Dundalk.

In 1926 'Sinn Féin Reorganised' split on the issue of the possibility of its members taking up seats in Dáil Éireann. Following the lead of de Valera, many members broke away and established Fianna Fáil, which they named 'The 'Republican Party'. On 16 February 1932 Fianna Fáil came into power with the support of Labour TDs. The new government released all IRA prisoners who had been interned during or after the Civil War and lifted the ban on the IRA and FÉ.

Subsequently members of these organisations were involved in the systematic intimidation of Cumann na nGaedhael representatives and supporters. A number of important Cumann na nGaedhael meetings were totally disrupted in September, October and November 1932 This led the Army Comrades Association (ACA), an organisation of Irish Free State army veterans, later popularly known as the Blueshirts, to attempt to protect meetings held by Cumann na nGaedhael. On 8 September 1933 Cumann na nGaedhael, the Centre Party and the National Guard/Blueshirts amalgamated to form a new party, which they named Fine Gael. The opposition of the IRA and FÉ to this new Party was almost fanatical. This was evident when Eoin O'Duffy, its leader, visited Tralee to address a meeting on 6 October 1933. The meeting was disrupted. O'Duffy was struck in the head with a hammer. His car was burnt. Many of his supporters were assaulted. Considerable damage was done to property. Later, over one hundred Fine Gael delegates were besieged in the hall by a stone-throwing crowd outside. A Mills bomb was thrown through the skylight over the stage but it did not explode and remained caught in the wire netting. Subsequently it became known that it was a sixteen-year old member of FÉ who had thrown the bomb, which could have had devastating consequences. The 200 unarmed police present were unable to cope with the rioting crowd. A burst of machine-gun fire was directed at their local barracks. It was only when soldiers arrived from Cork that some semblance of law and order was restored.

Not surprisingly the IRA and FÉ soon found themselves as much at odds with the Fianna Fáil government and its successors as they had been formerly with the Cumann na nGaedhael administrations. When the IRA launched a bombing campaign against Britain after the outbreak of World War II the Fianna Fáil government stood resolute and brought the full weight of the law to bear on them. Hundreds were interned and a number were executed. Among the latter was Charlie Kerins who had been an officer in the Tralee *sluagh* of FÉ. In the late 1930s and the 1940s the annual pilgrimage of Republicans to the grave of Wolfe Tone at Bodenstown was specifically banned. However, in spite of a large police and military presence, the Dublin brigade of FÉ continued each year the tradition of honouring the father of Irish republicanism.

In the early 1950s IRA and FÉ membership increased, which led to the beginning of the IRA's border campaign in 1956. This consisted of attacks on RUC barracks and public installations north of the border. Hundreds of members of the IRA and FÉ were interned on both sides of the border. The campaign received little public support and was called off in 1962 but not before Seán South, a former member of the Limerick *sluagh*, was killed in the course of an attack on Brookborough RUC barracks in County Fermanagh on New Year's Day 1957.

In August 1959 a committee composed of former members of FÉ organised a number of events to celebrate the golden jubilee of the organisation. They had a calvary and a plaque erected at the Retreat House of the Capuchin friars in Raheny, Dublin, in honour of Fr Albert, OFM Cap and Fr Dominic, OFM CAP, both of whom had been closely associated with FÉ during the War of Independence and in the Civil War. They also presented a ceilidhe and pageant in the Mansion House and published *Souvenir of the Golden Jubilee of Fianna Éireann*. The booklet included the following message from Éamon Martin, a former chief of staff:

Tonight we are gathered to commemorate the golden jubilee of Fianna Éireann and it is appropriate to take a brief look back. Fifty years ago when pride of nationhood was at its lowest ebb in Ireland we put our hands to a seemingly forlorn task. We had little else than faith and hope to aid us but after four years of hard persevering work, and withstanding jibes and sneers, we at last found reward. We were to see the men of Ireland organised into a Volunteer army pledged to the same object to which we had pledged ourselves and we were no longer alone. Thenceforward we marched side by side and the results of the Fianna's pioneer work became increasingly evident with the new-born resurgence spreading the length and breadth of the country. If a lesson is to be learned from this it is that a nation must ever place its reliance and hope on its youth.

On this fiftieth anniversary of the founding of our organisation we veteran members of Fianna Éireann welcome this gathering of young men and women, believing that they will faithfully carry on the traditions of our nation and confident that our aim – the independence of Ireland – shall be not less cherished in their young hearts. With that confidence we hand on our standard and we pass on to face our closing days, with complete and absolute content.

Inis an Ghlóir go raibh lóistin ag
Slóite na bhFiann

O'KELLY GROUP OF FÉ

The manifest failure of the IRA border campaign caused serious soul-searching and tensions within the republican movement. With the Sinn Féin-IRA leadership wishing to bow to the inevitable and end the campaign, an IRA splinter group, which remained more committed than the leadership to traditional physical-force republicanism, emerged.

In FÉ there was also tension and division at that time. In 1955 Thomas Conleth O'Kelly, also known as Gearóid Ó Ceallaigh, set up what became known as the 'O'Kelly group'. He had been deported from England in 1939 during the IRA bombing campaign in Britain. He remained associated with the IRA and Sinn Féin on his return and for many years was a member of FÉ. He served as chairman of the Austin Stack Cumann of Sinn Féin in Dublin in 1950. Subsequently he was entrusted with the task of organising a cumann in Newbridge, County Kildare. In 1955 he was expelled from Sinn Féin, owing to a disagreement with the *Comhairle Ceanntair* with regard to nominations for the local elections in the Newbridge electoral district. At loggerheads with Sinn Féin, he allied himself with the IRA splinter group. In 1955 he was Chief Scout of FÉ and opposed attempts by the stronger Sinn Féin-IRA group to exercise control over the organisation. The leader of a large *sluagh* centred on Blessington Street in Dublin, also at that time, he made it independent of Sinn Féin-IRA .

O'Kelly's north city *sluagh* survived for a number of years. But its meetings were occasionally disrupted and its members were subjected to harassment by other members of FÉ. O'Kelly was physically attacked and sought police protection on a number of occasions. On St Patrick's day 1958 he, as Chief Scout of FÉ, and his assistant, Michael J. McEvoy, as chief secretary, requested an interview with Archbishop John C. McQuaid with a view to having a chaplain appointed to their organisation. This prompted the archbishop to request Monsignor Michael O'Halloran to send him a report on O'Kelly and his organisation. With the assistance of Superintendent John MacMahon of the Garda Special Branch he submitted this and thereafter O'Kelly and McEvoy were informed that it was not usual to appoint a chaplain to an association unless it was of a religious or moral character and then only after its statutes had been examined and tested.

On 11 October 1958 O'Kelly attended a meeting at which all the officers of FÉ were present. Charges were brought against him, one of which was his failure to account for collection boxes and their contents. He was relieved of his position as Chief Scout, dismissed from FÉ and directed to return the organisation's property. Notwithstanding this, O'Kelly continued to claim to be and to act as Chief Scout. On 5 January 1959 Thomas Weldon, quarter-master of FÉ, and Thomas Phelan forced an entry into O'Kelly's home and, while threatening him with a revolver, took away his Chief Scout's uniform and other FÉ uniforms. O'Kelly brought charges against them. Weldon and Phelan were in court two weeks later and were sentenced to three months in prison. Fully aware of how seriously the republican movement regarded his actions in taking an internal dissension into the public legal forum, O'Kelly went 'on the run'. This ended his attempt to conduct the north city *sluagh* independently of the Sinn Féin-IRA leadership.

FRANK LEIGH'S IRISH NATIONAL BOY SCOUTS' ASSOCIATION
Also at this time another scout organisation with FÉ associations was set up. On 17 March 1959 Frank Leigh, a former Chief Scout of FÉ and a former trustee of its funds, together with Terry Kiely established the Irish National Boy Scouts' Association. The aim of the new association was stated to be 'education in the form of entertainment to provide better citizenship among youth'. Members of the new organisation wore a khaki uniform. The rest of their uniform differed from that of other scouting organisations in that the officers and senior scouts wore slacks and forage caps instead of the usual berets. It also had a distinctive badge.

In early June 1960 Leigh and Kiely approached Fr Michael Hayes, a curate in the parish of Milltown in South Dublin, seeking his assistance in establishing a troop in the area. When he suggested to them that they set up a Catholic Boy Scouts of Ireland (CBSI) troop they expressed their contempt for that association. Fr Hayes applied to a secretary in Archbishop's House for a direction on how to respond to their request. This prompted Archbishop John C. McQuaid to ask Fr Alfred Tonge, Dublin diocesan chaplain, CBSI, for a report on Frank Leigh and his organisation.

On 24 June Fr Tonge submitted the following report, which not only provided a profile of Leigh and his scout organisation but an insight into how FÉ was viewed in clerical circles at that time:

Frank Leigh of Haddington Road, a son of a Civic Guard, was and most probably still is an active member of the new IRA. His National Scout movement stems from Fianna Éireann. He was an active member of the Fianna until he fell out of favour over a dispute about missing funds and so he has started his own scouts. His aims in recruiting and training the boys are no different from those of Fianna Éireann. At most his group would number about thirty boys.

Fianna Éireann proper is a youth movement actively organised and possessed by the new IRA. At most they would have one hundred members in the different districts of the Dublin area; more likely less. They can normally only organise in districts where there are no troops of CBSI because parents question their children as to why they should be in a scout movement other than that run by the local clergy. The Fianna Éireann is a scout movement in the technical sense and is looked upon as a means of recruiting for the active IRA. The boys are taught Irish history with the IRA bias and trained keenly in drill; active adventure scouting which appeals very much to the boys and when they go on camp often their leader carries a .22 rifle. The IRA look upon the Fianna as their only body which can wear uniform in public and so is a kind of advertisement for them. They can keep their boys to a later age than most youth movements and the aim is to entice their boys around the ages of seventeen and eighteen to join the militant IRA which is the whole purpose of Fianna Éireann in the eyes of the leaders.

Frank Leigh had a meeting with Fianna Éireann with a view to possible re-amalgamation...

In July 1961 Fr Tonge again reported to the archbishop on the organisation of Frank Leigh, whom he described as an 'ex-IRA Chief Scout'. By the end of that year Leigh had established four troops. At Bray there was a troop numbering about twenty, at Ballyfermot a troop numbering about sixty, at Milltown a troop also numbering about twenty and the most successful was one at Sandymount. It had about eighty members. Leigh had a flair for generating good publicity. In early March 1962 he discussed his scout organisation on RTÉ's television programme *Broadcast*. When pressed by the presenter, John O'Donoghue, as to whether or not his organisation had any military significance or implications, he refused to give an unequivocal answer. Reports in the *Evening Herald* recorded the progress of the new scout organisation. In the issue of 3 March 1962 it was stated that a new scouts' headquarters and hall was to be built in Sandymount, the Ballyfermot troop was to travel to Scotland for their annual camp and the

Sandymount troop were to have a stay at a summer camp at Stuttgart. In the issue of 7 March it was reported that an elite group of the Sandymount scouts named the Pioneer Corps had been trained in forest-warden activities' and were to take part in the St Patrick's Day parade.

Not all of Leigh's more ambitious plans were realised. However the flurry of publicity prompted another report to the archbishop from Fr Tonge, dated 16 March 1962. This was much more favourable than his previous reports. It stated that Leigh 'is neither involved in IRA activities nor a communist even though he calls his flag 'The Red Star' from the fact that it contained thirty-two stars to represent the thirty-two counties'. The report continued that there was nothing wrong or subversive about his organisation. Monsignor Cecil Barrett who was also asked by the archbishop for an opinion on Leigh wrote on 12 June 1962 that there was no evidence of wrongdoing against Leigh and that he was 'looked upon more as a scout fanatic'. He suggested that, if required, competition from the CBSI might well prove to be the best antidote to his activities.

By 1963 Leigh was still not able to settle his dispute with the FÉ leadership with regard to his alleged malfeasance when acting as trustee of their funds. As a result it became increasingly inadvisable for him to remain in Dublin. He had a genuine concern for the future wellbeing of his troops and their membership. Thus he had lengthy informal discussions with James Nolan, national secretary of the CBSI, with a view to having his organisation amalgamated into that association. These discussions, however, proved to be inconclusive.

REORGANISATION

In the early 1960s FÉ reorganised and embarked on an intensive recruiting campaign particularly in the nationalist areas of Northern Ireland but also in the Republic. Thus at this time there was a flourishing troop centred on 'The Ranch', a housing scheme in the Ballyfermot district. In 1963 its monthly *Fianna* reappeared and in the following year *The Young Guard of Erin*, an updated edition of the handbook, was published. At that time also the department of associate membership was revived. This had been established in 1912. Its purpose was to give moral support to FÉ, to organise fundraising events, and to help with recruitment. In addition efforts were made to increase membership of a sister organisation, *Cumann na gCailiní*: Irish National Girl Scouts. It had been set up in the early 1930s. Open to Irish girls over seven years of age, its object was: 'To foster in the minds of Irish girls a desire for the complete freedom of their country and a concern for the welfare of its people, that they may be prepared to take their place in a free and Gaelic Ireland.' This was to be achieved: 'By educating them in the history, language and culture of their country and by practising the principles and exercise of scouting'.

LURCH TO THE LEFT

While this activity continued at grassroots level, the leadership of the republican movement was taking a lurch to the left. In so doing it was influenced by events outside the country as well as within it. In the US the civil rights movement led by the Reverend Martin Luther King showed how a non-violent movement concentrating on the need for social reform could win civil rights and successfully oppose repression. The Anti-Apartheid Movement in South Africa, which for the most part was non-violent, taught a similar lesson.

Nearer home there was the Campaign for Social Justice in Northern Ireland. Launched by Dr Conn McCluskey and his wife Patricia in January 1964, it directed attention in Britain to social injustice in Northern Ireland and to this end accumulated data on discrimination in housing, employment, electoral practices and public appointments. It worked in association with the British Labour Party, the British Council for Civil Liberties and the Campaign for Democracy in Ulster, founded by British Labour Party MPs in 1965. It evolved into that much larger Northern Ireland Civil Rights Association in 1967. Both were committed to non-violent action in their efforts to secure equality of treatment and parity of esteem for all the citizens of Northern Ireland.

In the meantime in 1959 republican leaders had been dismayed by the fiasco that was the IRA border campaign. Among them was Cathal Goulding. In the 1930s he was a member of the same FÉ *sluagh* as Brendan Behan and in the 1940s they were again colleagues in the IRA. In 1961 Goulding was quartermaster of the IRA. Two years later he was its chief of staff. At that time also the single-minded left-leaning Seán Garland was secretary of Sinn Féin. Neither needed much persuading to lead the republican movement to the left. Among those eager to persuade them was Roy Johnston. A science graduate of Trinity College, Dublin, he was employed by the Guinness company in England. On returning to Ireland in 1963 he joined Sinn Féin and the IRA. In that year also he was co-founder of the Wolfe Tone Society, the aim of which he stated as: 'to work out a synthesis between the traditional republican population and socialism'. From 1965 onwards he was education officer for the Republican Movement. A life-long communist from the age of seventeen, he availed of every opportunity to introduce a Marxist perspective and Marxist principles into the republican movement.

C. Desmond Greaves was also influential in this regard. A life-long member of the Communist Party of Great Britain, he was a prominent member of the left-leaning Connolly Association in Britain and for forty years editor of its monthly *The Irish Democrat*. He was tireless in his efforts to bring the injustices of partition to the attention of the British Labour movement. He urged that the 'Irish problem' be solved peacefully by ending the social disparity and inequalities between nationalists and unionists. His approach, he argued, would be successful as it would convince the moderate section of unionists to realise that there was no longer any rationale or real advantage in retaining partiion. Anthony C. Coughlan also contributed to the politicisation of the republican movement at that time. He had served as a full-time organiser for the Connolly Association in 1960–2. On his return to Ireland he became a lecturer in the department of social studies in Trinity College, Dublin, and was a frequent lecturer at republican gatherings. He was a member neither of the Communist Party nor of Sinn Féin, nor of the IRA but an independent-minded commentator and prominent member and eventually secretary of the Wolfe Tone Society. He argued for a republican-left convergence' and the adoption of a political rather than a military campaign to end partition.

The 'republican-left' convergence was not popular with many in the rank and file of the republican movement. This was especially so with most members of FÉ. They were singularly unimpressed when in 1965-6 they were informed that their organisation was to be radically changed from a scouting association into a youth movement. To this end it was proposed that FÉ would be disbanded and subsequently absorbed into the leftist 'Connolly Youth Movement'. This proposal and a consequent directive to implement it were ignored.

SPLIT IN REPUBLICAN MOVEMENT

The majority of unionists were resolute in their opposition to the civil rights campaign. Some organised counter-demonstrations and attacked civil rights supporters. On 5 October 1968 a rally in Derry, organised by the Northern Ireland Civil Rights Association, was banned by the minister for home affairs. It went ahead and in front of TV cameras the RUC savagely batoned the marchers off the streets. On 9 October students from Queen's University, Belfast, demonstrated in the city for civil rights and formed what became known as the People's Democracy. On 4 January 1969 a civil rights march across Northern Ireland by this organisation had to be abandoned when it was violently attacked by loyalists at Burntollet, County Derry, as members of the RUC stood by. On 19 April civil rights supporters were attacked by a loyalist mob in Derry. Subsequently these loyalists and members of the RUC ran riot in the nationalist Bogside area of the city. On 11 August the 'Battle of the Bogside' began as loyalists, the RUC and the Ulster Special Constabulary (the B-Specials, a Protestant paramilitary ancillary police-force) stormed into the nationalist area of Derry. Fianna boys were among those withstanding the assault.

In the following days the situation deteriorated further. On 14–15 August, provoked by rioting nationalists, loyalists and the B-Specials attacked nationalist areas in Belfast. They torched over 150 homes of nationalists between the Shankhill Road and the Divis district. The mob then closed in on the local Catholic school and the Clonard monastery of the Redemptorists. The local community, with the help of a handful of armed members of the IRA, succeeded in holding them off until elements of the British army eventually arrived. Members of the local *sluagh* of FÉ were involved in the attempts to defend their community and neighbourhood. One of them, Gerard McAuley, was among the six fatal casualties of the pogrom.

The pogroms and riots caused thousands of Northern nationalists to flee to the Republic where the Irish army provided field hospitals for shelter. The Taoiseach, Jack Lynch, in a national broadcast announced that the government would not stand by while innocent people were attacked because of their religion. Northern nationalists were not reassured by his words. On the one hand they were aware how limited his help had to be and on the other they had been shocked at how ineffectual the IRA, their traditional defenders, had been at that time.

By the end of the 1960s the Republican-left convergence put Sinn Féin in control of the republican movement and the IRA practically moribund. Cathal Goulding was chief of staff of a secret army with few members and even fewer arms. Northern nationalists made emotional appeals for help. Before the end of the year sympathisers south of the border provided them with guns and money. This was to facilitate the creation of the Provisional IRA. Also in the charged atmosphere at that time recruitment to the IRA and FÉ was unprecedented in the nationalist areas of Northern Ireland. The outbreak of civil unrest and rioting in Northern Ireland in August 1969 pushed the tension between those for and against the mingling of socialism with traditional republican ideology beyond breaking point. In December the army council of the IRA split on the symbolic issue of parliamentary abstention, with the dissident minority forming the Provisional army council and choosing Seán Mac Stíofáin as chief of staff. The majority later became known as the 'Official IRA'. This split was replicated at the Sinn Féin *ardfheis* on 4 January 1970 when a third of the delegates gave their allegiance to the Povisional movement The division in the republican movement was primarily a Belfast–Dublin split with the Provisionals mainly dominated by Belfast republicans and the Officials led from Dublin. At that time most *sluaighte* of FÉ and those with the highest membership were in Northern Ireland, so with few exceptions FÉ transferred their allegiance to the new Provisional IRA movement.

CHAPTER FIVE

The Last Phase

GUERRILLA WAR

THE RUMP OF THE PRE-1970 republican movement continued as Official Sinn Féin and the Official IRA. Official Sinn Féin was led initially by Tomás Mac Giolla. It subsequently became Sinn Féin: the Workers' Party, later the Workers' Party, and later still Democratic Left, until eventually in 1991 it was, in large part, absorbed into the Labour Party. The Official IRA was led by Cathal Goulding. Until 1972 it was involved in sporadic fighting with the Provisional IRA, the RUC, the British army and the Irish Republican Socialist Party (IRSP). Thereafter it continued only in the guise of the republican clubs in Belfast.

The Provisional IRA went from strength to strength. In their weekly *An Phoblacht* they declared that their aim was not merely to defend the nationalist areas of Northern Ireland but to end the British occupation of the six counties. At that time many in the republican movement viewed the oncoming conflict as the last phase in the struggle for independence. By mid-June the Provisional IRA was estimated to have had 1,500 active volunteers. Of these, 800 were in Northern Ireland, 600 in Belfast, 100 in Derry and 100 in other nationalist areas. Many of the most committed activists were former members of FÉ. The initial support in arms and finance from the Republic was supplemented by arms and ammunition smuggled in from Britain and the continent of Europe and financed by Irish-American sympathisers through Northern Aid. From June 1970 onwards the Provisional IRA engaged the British security forces and their war of attrition continued until July 1997, apart from ceasefires in 1974–5 and 1994–6.

On 9 August 1971, in a determined effort to break the Provisional IRA, the Northern Ireland government introduced internment without trial. Hundreds of residents in the Catholic nationalist areas were arrested and interned by the RUC and the British army. In anticipation of the raids, most of the Provisional IRA activists had fled to the Republic. Many of those interned were not associated in any way with the republican movement. Seventeen people were killed and thousands of Catholics fled across the border, where they were housed in army camps. As was subsequently disclosed at the European Court of Human Rights, some of these arrested were subjected to torture ('degrading and inhuman treatment') by joint British army–RUC interrogation teams. The implementation of internment by the British alienated the entire nationalist population in Northern Ireland and boosted membership of the Provisional IRA. At that time members of FÉ who were not assisting with IRA operations were active in anti-British propaganda and in fomenting anti-British resentment in the nationalist population.

Anti-British feeling spread to the Republic following the incidents on 'Bloody Sunday'. On that day, 30 January 1972, British paratroopers fired on a banned civil rights march in Derry and thirteen unarmed civil rights marchers were shot dead, with another dying later of his wounds. On 2 February after a protest march by a huge crowd, some elements, which the Garda Síochána were unable to contain, set fire to the British Embassy in Dublin in retaliation for the Bloody Sunday deaths in Derry. The Widgery inquiry established by the British government to inquire into the Bloody Sunday killings reported on 19 April. The attempt by the inquiry and the British government to justify the atrocity further inflamed Irish public opinion. All elements of the republican movement, including FÉ, were active in ensuring that the high level of emotion at that time was sustained. In addition FÉ took part in demonstrations which were organised to place pressure on the Irish government to become involved in the conflict in Northern Ireland.

Throughout 1972 the situation in Northern Ireland deteriorated further. Loyalist attacks against isolated Catholics and Catholic neighbourhoods intensified following the introduction of direct rule from London. When the army and RUC announced early in July that they were to take control of all areas of Northern Ireland, over 7,000 people fled across the border to the Republic. The expected increase in violence was not long in coming. On 21 July, 'Bloody Friday', twenty-six Provisional IRA bombs in Belfast killed eleven and injured 130 people, most of them civilian. Four days later the British army and RUC stormed into nationalist 'no-go' areas. During the upsurge of violence there were frequent clashes between the security forces and the Provisional IRA on the streets of Belfast and Derry. This was the bloodiest year of the conflict with 496 deaths, including members of the British army, RUC, Provisional IRA and many civilians. The fighting also claimed the lives of twelve members of FÉ.

CONFRONTATION IN THE PRISONS

The Provisional IRA conducted their campaign against the British authorities in the prisons as well as outside them. In June 1972 the Provisional IRA prisoners demanded political status. When this was refused they began a strike to achieve it. On 21 June the secretary of state for Northern Ireland, William Whitelaw, allowed Republican prisoners to have special category status. This, in effect, recognised them as prisoners of war. In return the Provisional IRA leaders agreed to meet him. In the event, the meeting, which was held in London, was inconclusive, as the Provisionals were prepared to discuss only the outline of a phased withdrawal of the British from Northern Ireland.

The issue of political status or special category status for Provisional IRA prisoners became a flashpoint again in September 1976 when it was withdrawn from Republican prisoners in Long Kesh, the Maze Prison. The prisoners refused to wear the supplied prison clothes and began the 'blanket protest campaign'. The 'blanket campaign' was followed by the 'dirty protest' when from March 1978 prisoners refused to wash or use toilet facilities and soiled the walls of their cells.

The prisoners' issue became particularly acute when on 27 October 1980 these protests in the H-Block of the prison developed into a hunger strike. A number of unsuccessful attempts were made to have it called off. During 1981 ten of the hunger strikers died. Each of the deaths aided recruitment to the Provisional IRA and created a fraught atmosphere in Northern Ireland. The hunger strike ended on 2 October 1981 although the prisoners were granted only a small number of their demands. Most of the prisoners in H-Block were former members of FÉ, including Raymond McCreesh, Patsy O'Hare and Kieran Doherty who died on the hunger strike. From the start of the prisoners' protest in 1976 until it ended in 1981 members of FÉ were particularly active in mobilising the support of young people behind the prisoners' demands. To that end it organised 'Youth Against H-Block' groups. In addition, members were present at marches, demonstrations, protest meetings and occupations to focus attention on the plight of the republican prisoners. By virtue of Section 31 of the Emergency Powers Act of 1976 republican propaganda was censored by RTÉ. FÉ members regularly protested against this policy in the 1970s and 1980s. Some of their protests were spectacular, such as climbing and displaying placards on the RTÉ mast at Montrose, Donnybrook.

A POLITICAL STRATEGY EMERGES

Ironically it was when the impasse in Northern Ireland appeared to be most intractable that the seeds of resolution were sown. The H-block hunger strike of 1981 further deepened the conflict and gave rise to dramatic public support for the hunger strikers. Sinn Féin benefited from the upsurge in support for the republican cause among nationalists and became a real political force for the first time. Gerry Adams was the main beneficiary of this development. Even though the Catholic hierarchy urged nationalists not to vote for those who supported Provisional IRA violence, he defeated Gerry Fitt to become the abstentionist MP for West Belfast in June 1983.

Adams, an important figure in the republican movement in Belfast, had been interned from 1973 to 1977. While in the Maze prison, under the pen name 'Brownie', he published a series of articles in *Republican News* in which he outlined a strategy which would enable the Provisional IRA to build a political structure through Sinn Féin while pursuing an armed struggle. Adams and Martin McGuinness took control of Sinn Féin in November 1983. Thereafter they used their influence to impose this new policy gradually across the republican movement. It was described by Sinn Féin director of publicity Danny Morrison as going forward 'with the armalite in one hand and the ballot box in the other'. In accordance with the new policy from this time onwards FÉ's *sluaighte* in Belfast, Derry, Newry, Strabane and elsewhere in Northern Ireland were no longer to be regarded as paramilitary but rather as political units of the republican movement.

The conflict continued on its tragic course for another ten years. But war weariness set in. The Provisional IRA realised that they could not bomb unionists into a united Ireland. The British government acknowledged that it could not defeat the IRA militarily, mainly because of the restraints imposed by virtue of its being a liberal democratic administration. And a substantial majority of unionists came to terms with the fact that unless they conceded, as a mantra of the time put it, 'equality of rights and parity of esteem' to their fellow-citizens in the Catholic, nationalist, republican communities, Northern Ireland would not have a worthwhile future.

In this atmosphere Adams, president of Sinn Féin, and John Hume, leader of the Social Democratic and Labour Party (SDLP), held secret talks in January 1988. They were attempting to work out an agreement which would pave the way for peace. As an essential element of the peace process, Hume insisted that the IRA abandon violence and seek a constitutional solution to the Northern problem. These talks resumed in April 1993. This prompted Albert Reynolds, the Taoiseach, and John Major, the British prime minister, to pursue their own discussions. As part of those, Reynolds and Major issued the Downing Street Declaration in London in December 1993. While it guaranteed the position of Northern Ireland in the United Kingdom, it allowed for the creation of a united Ireland if a majority of people within Northern Ireland and the Republic voted to unify the country. The talks between Hume and Adams continued into the multi-party talks of the Northern Ireland Forum. Eventually the Belfast Agreement, also known as the Good Friday Agreement, was signed in April 1998. The Agreement was endorsed by referenda north and south of the border on 22 May 1998. When it was revealed that more than 71 per cent of voters supported the agreement in Northern Ireland and 95 per cent voted for it in the Republic there were manifestations of relief and joy across the whole island.

DECLINE OF FIANNA ÉIREANN

These developments spelled the beginning of the end of FÉ, as did the fact that in the 1980s and 1990s so many of those who were active in the republican movement were in prison north and south of the border. At the FÉ *Ardfheis* in October 1983 it was claimed that the organisation had 600 members. However the vast majority of these were no longer active and were merely members in name only as most *sluaighte* had become moribund. A Department of Training which had been particularly active in the early 1970s was no longer 'effective'. To facilitate reorganisation and recruitment, the *Ardfheis* amended the constitution to lessen the military aspect of FÉ.

The next *Ardfheis* was held in March 1987. Reports indicated the continuing decline of the organisation. To help reverse it, the *Ardfheis* decided to have the handbook updated. *Fianna Éireann Handbook: Lámhleabhar Fianna Éireann,* by Pádraig Mac Fhloinn was published in 1988. The traditional activities of FÉ *sluaighte* remained the same. In their own area they took part in ceremonies marking the Easter Rising. Members also provided a colour party for the annual republican commemoration at Bodenstown each June. FÉ members continued to take part in commemorations, demonstrations, marches and protests organised by the republican movement. The 'patriot dead' were also remembered during educational visits to Glasnevin Cemetery, Kilmainham Jail, St Enda's school and the 1916 section of the National Museum of Ireland.

By the mid-1980s the number of people in Ireland who were prepared to cast a tolerant eye on an organisation that indoctrinated children and boys and girls in extreme nationalism had greatly diminished. There were fewer parents than ever before who would encourage their children to join FÉ. Nor did the persistent harassment of leaders and members by the Special Branch of the Garda Síochána in the Republic and by the RUC in Northern Ireland help recruitment.

After the historic Good Friday Agreement in 1998, while some *sluaighte* survived in nationalist areas of Northern Ireland, the well-nigh terminal decline of those in the Republic was inevitable.

Memorandum No 1
Fianna Éireann

G.H.QRS. Dublin, 1921

To each Fianna officer,

A Chara,

As a result of conversations between the ministry of defence and Fianna General H.Q. Staff, the Fianna has now been recognised as one of the units at the disposal of the Republican government. This means that the Fianna will assist the I.V. [Irish Volunteers] in every manner possible under our own officers, and though acting in cooperation with the I.V. will remain in most respects a separate organisation. The connecting link between the I.V. and Fianna will be the liaison officer. The following will explain how the scheme affects *sluaighte* or companies:

(1) The Fianna shall assist, when required, the army of Ireland in operations. Such company or unit will work under its own officer who will be responsible to the I.V. officer in charge of operations.

(2) Fianna battalion areas will correspond with those of the I.V. Each battalion will have its battalion comdt. who will give instructions to the various companies. The Fianna battalion comdt. will be responsible for the carrying out of certain operations to the I.V. battalion comdt. (or brigade comdt.) and to Fianna G.H.Q. only. This means that all instructions from I.V. to Fianna come from I.V. brigade comdt. or battalion comdt. to Fianna battalion comdt. who will transmit them to unite in his command.

(3) The Fianna battalion comdt. will keep constantly in touch with battalion H.Q. of I.V. and will be summoned when necessary to I.V. brigade or battalion council meetings. In other words he will be the connecting link, or liaison officer, between Fianna and I.V. In cases where there is no Fianna battalion comdt. the senior Fianna officer will act as liaison offi-

cer, until such time as battalion strength will have been reached.

(4) Where the Fianna organisation is incomplete the I.V. will organise companies or Fianna, placing a section leader of I.V. in charge until such time as the company may be sufficiently organised to elect their own officer.

(5) On attaining the age of 18 a boy, unless his services are necessary for the successful management of the company, will be transferred to the I.V. Such transfers must be made in writing and countersigned by the Fianna battalion comdt. These transfers which are of the greatest importance must be made regularly, and a record must be kept in each company of such transfers.

TRAINING

Arrangements are being made whereby selected members of the Fianna (officers and boys) shall attend I.V. officers' and section commanders' classes. Circulars on training in special branches will be issued by G.H.Q. in due course.

In the meantime each O/C will immediately train the boys in despatch carrying (including correctly delivering verbal messages), Morse signals and reconnaissance. Specially selected boys of good physique can be trained where opportunities are available in bombing, rifle exercises, etc. The Fianna must supply trained men to Ireland's army. Intelligence work may be also included in the programme of training. This must be done carefully and with the sanction of the I.V. battalion comdt.

OPERATIONS

The Fianna must not carry out operations without having previously obtained (through Fianna battalion comdt.) sanction from I.V. battalion comdt. This will prevent overlapping and extra work.

REPORTS

Regular monthly reports must be sent by each O/C. They can, until regular battalion areas are defined, be sent direct to G.H.Qrs.

COMMUNICATIONS

As the British post is unsatisfactory and dangerous, arrangements are being made with I.V. G.H.Qrs. to make use of the I.V. lines of communication. Care should be taken that no frivolous correspondence is sent through these lines. Only urgent and necessary communications should be forwarded in this manner. Interview with battalion comdt. I.V. on this matter.

GENERAL

The intention of G.H.Qrs. Fianna is to make the Fianna a live organisation. G.H.Q. has been recognised and will give you every assistance possible. We must supply the trained man-power for Ireland's fight. Officers will thus realise the importance of enforcing discipline, and organising and training their boys. Let us work for Ireland.

ON FOR FREEDOM, FIANNA ÉIREANN

(Signed)
BARNEY MELLOWS,
Adjt.-General

PART III

Catholic Boy Scouts of Ireland

Towards a Catholic Boy Scout Association
The Early Years
Era of Fr Tom Farrell
World War II and Thereafter
Towards Unification

CHAPTER ONE

Towards a Catholic Boy Scout Association

END OF CIVIL WAR

THE CIVIL WAR between those who accepted and those who rejected the Anglo-Irish Treaty ended in May 1923 with the defeat of the anti-Treatyites. For the most part members of Fianna Éireann had supported the anti-Treatyites during the conflict. In its immediate aftermath there was a general consensus that it was imperative to ensure that boys and young men should no longer join political or militarist organisations and that it was necessary to provide alternative organisations for young people and to this end a number of initiatives were taken.

CATHOLIC BOYS BRIGADE

On 12 November 1924 a branch of the Catholic Boys Brigade for South County Dublin was established in Ballsbridge. Three days later the organisers requested Archbishop Edward Byrne to appoint a chaplain to the brigade into which, they stated the hope, they would enrol 200 boys from a number of parishes and 'make them a credit to the Catholic religion and Ireland'. One branch of the organisation had already been established in Dublin in March 1894 at a premises in Church Street. Four years later it had over 700 members. Its object was stated to be: 'To crush vice and evil habits amongst boys; to instruct them thoroughly in the Catholic doctrine; to prepare them for the worthy reception of the Sacraments; to give them habits of obedience, discipline and self-respect; reverence and love for ecclesiastical authority and our holy religion; to promote their moral, physical and temporal wellbeing; and to give them habits of strict sobriety'. While this branch flourished for another thirty-five years, the branch at Ballsbridge was did not survive for more than a few years.

CLANNA FODHLA

On 3 October 1925 a group referring to themselves as the committee of Clanna Fodhla and with an address at 28 South Frederick Street wrote to Archbishop Byrne informing him that they had established a scout movement which they described as 'thoroughly Catholic in ideal, and non-political in fact and in name'. Its main object, they stated, was to 'make good citizens' which could best be 'achieved by attracting boys into an organisation which kept them morally straight, mentally awake and physically strong'. It seems that during the previous three months the committee had enrolled 500 boys into the movement in Dublin and had set up *clanna* or troops in Cork, Galway and Glandore, County Cork. They were currently doing the same in places in County Offaly. The committee forwarded a brochure with details of the organisation's constitution and requested the archbishop to appoint a chaplain to the movement. In the brochure the new organisation was described as 'Clanna Fodhla: Irish National Scouts' but significantly in a brochure belatedly sent to the archbishop a week later it was described as 'Clanna Fodhla: Irish National Catholic Scouts'.

On being informed that a chaplain could not be appointed to an organisation unless it had been approved by the hierarchy, the committee forwarded the constitution of Clanna Fodhla: Irish National Catholic Scouts and other material to the archbishop on 31 December 1925 with a request that the matter be submitted to the next meeting of the hierarchy with a view to having the movement approved. In the event the archbishop inquired into the background of the leaders of the new movement and concluded that it was set to be far more nationalist than it would be Catholic. It seems that some of the leaders were members of Fianna Éireann who had not taken part in the Civil War and others were well-known republicans. The movement did not receive episcopal approval and within a few years some of its members had rejoined Fianna Éireann. Others ome established a troop of Catholic Boy Scouts at Fairview, Dublin, and many of the rest eventually joined the Catholic Boy Scouts of Ireland on its establishment.

CALLS FOR A CATHOLIC BOY SCOUT ORGANISATION

James J. Pakenham was an early advocate of the need for a Catholic boy scout organisation. Over the *nom-de-plume* 'Old Camper', he published articles on camping in *Our Boys* – the popular magazine published each fortnight by the Christian Brothers – of 28 May, 4 June, 16 July and 17 August 1925. In the issue of 4 June he suggested that there should be a Catholic boy scout organisation. Over the *nom-de-plume* 'A Priest', Fr Ernest Farrell was far less tentative in *Our Boys* of 1 October and 12 November. He extolled the merits of scouting and, in effect, pleaded with the bishops to sanction the establishment of a countrywide Catholic scouting organisation. On 12 November he stated that since his previous article 'a large number of letters of approval' had been received and many also had 'appeared in the press'. In the issue of 26 November Fr Farrell drew attention to the strong support of the pope for the Catholic scout movement on the continent. This issue also carried a letter from Thomas Markham, described as 'Chairman, Clanna Fodhla', endorsing 'A priest's' call for an Irish scout movement 'Catholic in ideal and non-political in fact and in name'. Articles promoting the idea of a Catholic scout association appeared in the *Irish Catholic* of 28 November and the *Leader* of 5 and 12 December 1925. Those in the *Leader* emphasised the necessity of the proposed boy scout organisation being non-military and non-political. The emphasis in 'The scout movement and Catholicity' by 'Dundealgan' (Fr Glendon, OP) which appeared in *Our Boys* of 7 January 1926, was on the importance of the proposed organisation being Catholic in name and in fact, and under episcopal supervision.

FR ERNEST AND FR TOM FARRELL

These brothers are regarded as the founders of the CBSI. Ernest, the younger, was ordained in June 1917. He served as a curate in Greystones, County Wicklow, from 1924 to 1927. While in the parish he was chaplain to a boys' club. He became immensely interested in scouting and acquired from the Boy Scouts of America their *Handbook* and other materials. In summer he took the boys on hikes and even organised occasional weekend camps. In 1925 and 1926, apart from campaigning in *Our Boys* for the establishment of a Catholic scout organisation, he was meeting like-minded laymen to this end. Ernest's brother, Tom, who was ordained in May 1907, served as a curate in the Pro-Cathedral parish from 1920 onwards, becoming its administrator in late 1939. He followed with interest the activities of his brother's 'scout group' in Greystones. He had also made himself familiar with the printed material on the Boy Scouts of America and was convinced of the benefit of scouting and the crucial need, especially at this time, to establish an Irish national Catholic scout organisation.

KNIGHTS OF ST COLUMBANUS

Both the Farrells were acutely aware that the approval of the hierarchy was a prerequisite for the establishment of a national Catholic boy scout organisation. They also realised that the most effective way of acquiring this was an appeal to this end made by influential Catholic laymen. As a curate in the Pro-Cathedral parish Fr Tom acted as chaplain to the Catholic Commercial Club in nearby O'Connell Street, where members of the Knights of St Columbanus frequently met. This order had been founded in Belfast in 1915 by Canon James O'Neill with the aim of cherishing 'fraternal charity and to develop practical Christianity among its members'. Branches were founded in Dublin in 1917 and in Cork in 1919. Its members were drawn for the most part from the professional and business classes. Several were active in the charitable work and devotional life of their own parishes. They also attempted to counter the excessive influence of freemasons in the business and commercial life of the country. Although they had to wait until 1934 for formal recognition from the Catholic Church, many of the members were among the most prominent lay Catholics of that time. Typical was Sir Joseph A. Glynn. He was a confidant of a number of the bishops and a much-sought-after and tireless supporter of various charities, fundraising for the missions and served as president from 1933 to 1939 of the St Joseph's Young Priests Society, an organisation to promote and foster vocations to the priesthood and religious life.

ORGANISING COUNCIL OF CBSI

Fr Tom Farrell, who was friendly with members of the Knights, and his brother Ernest had little difficulty in persuading some of them to form an organising committee for the establishment of a national Catholic boy scout organisation. By this time the Knights had become convinced of the merits and the need for such an organisation. Sir Joseph A. Glynn became chairman of the committee which was termed the organising council of the Catholic Boy Scouts of Ireland. Other members of the Knights served on it, together with Fr Ernest and Fr Tom Farrell, who acted as the Council's honorary secretary. The Council appointed a sub-committee, which included the Frs Farrell, to draft a constitution for a proposed Catholic Boy Scouts of Ireland. The constitution was drafted by the Farrells, using Boy Scouts of America documentation and with the advice of colleagues, not least Fr Michael Cronin, parish priest of Rathgar and former professor of ethics at University College, Dublin.

CATHOLIC BOY SCOUTS OF IRELAND ORGANISATION

Frs Ernest and Tom Farrell then prepared a synopsis of the constitution and other relevant material, to be incorporated in a handbook and sent these to

16. Countess Constance Markievicz. She founded Fianna Éireann in 1909

17. Bulmer Hobson, president of Fianna Éireann in 1909

18. Members of Fianna Éireann at Belcamp Park, Raheny, County Dublin, in 1910. *Front, middle*: Con Colbert

19. Fourth Fianna Éireann Ardfheis at Mansion House, Dublin, 13 July 1913. Countess Markievich is in the centre with Liam Mellows on her right and Pádraig Ó Riain and Con Colbert on her left

20. Members of Fianna Éireann with trek cart at the gun-running at Howth, 26 July 1914

21. Members of Fianna Éireann on a training routine in 1915

22. Officers of Fianna Éireann who took part in the Easter Rising 1916. *Left to right*: Eamon Martin, Gary Holohan

24. (Below) Joe McKelvey, commandant of Belfast battalion of Fianna Éireann 1921-22.

25. (Below right) Charlie Kerins, a former leader of the Tralee battalion of Fianna Éireann who, when OC, IRA, was executed on 1 December 1944

23. (Above) Liam Mellows, organiser of Fianna Éireann in 1911

26. Cumann na gCailíní: Irish National Girl Scouts on parade, *c.* 1957

27. Fianna Éireann leading the procession to Bodenstown in 1959

28. (Above) Golden Jubilee Committee at Mansion House on 26 July 1959. *Front row, left to right*: Séamus Pounch, Cathal O'Shannon, Eamon Martin, Harry Walpole, Jimmy O'Connor. *Second row, left to right*: Eugene Kelly, Christy Moore, Paddy O'Neill, Séamus Kavanagh. *Back row, left to right*: Christie Keogh, Peter Sinclair, Michael Kelly, Liam Timmins, Seán Brady, Joseph Valentine, Kit Martin

29. Uniforms of junior scout, senior scout, junior officer and senior officer of Fianna Éireann

30. 2nd Dublin, the Carmelite troop at Clarendon Street, when visited by Frs Tom and Ernest Farrell, *c.* 1929. *Front row, left to right*: Séamus O'Higgins, Fr Tom Farrell, Fr Stanislaus, OCD, Fr Ernest Farrell, Joe Carey

31. Chief Scout John O'Neill leads a party of commissioners in the Blessed Sacrament procession during the Lourdes pilgrimage in 1930. *Behind the torch-bearer: left to right*: Chief Scout John O'Neill, Commissioners Cameron Keelan, Dr Conor Martin, Ernest Cullen

32. *Top left*: Dr Conor Martin, national commissioner in the 1930s and medical supervisor of CBSI first-aid contingent at Eucharistic Congress in 1932. *Top right*: William Kinsella, deputy organiser of the Eucharistic Congress camp at Terenure College, later organiser of the first Dublin diocesan camp at Santry Park in 1937 and subsequently vice-president of the CBSI Association. *Bottom*: Mealtime at the camp. The chaplain serving the dinner is Fr D.J. Donovan of the Bandon troop, later vicar general of Cork diocese

each of the twenty-seven members of the Irish hierarchy. The synopsis was as follows:

CATHOLIC BOY SCOUTS OF IRELAND ORGANISATION

A scout troop is formed by a responsible local committee, or by a school. The committee consists of men over twenty-one years of age. The committee is responsible for the appointment of the scoutmaster, subject to the approval of the chaplain. It also takes charge of the finances of the troop, and manages the business side of the work.

Scouts are divided into:

(a) Scouts aged twelve to seventeen

(b) Knights errant seventeen upwards

A patrol consists of not more than eight scouts.

A troop consists of two or more patrols and is under a scoutmaster and assistant scoutmaster.

Each troop has a chaplain.

A district council consists of two or more troop committees. The district council deals with the scoutmasters, and all questions of exams for awards of honours, badges, etc. This is done through a court of honour appointed by the district council.

Diocesan councils are formed by two representatives from each troop. One of the two representatives must be the troop chaplain. The bishop is ex-officio chairman of the diocesan council and appoints the diocesan chaplain.

The diocesan council appoints a diocesan commissioner, who is over the scoutmasters of the diocese. The diocesan chaplain and diocesan commissioner are recognised by the national council.

The national council is the supreme ruling body and issues commissions to all diocesan commissioners, scout assistants, scoutmasters; awards honours and promotions, and issues charters to each troop and district council. It is maintained by affiliation fees and subscriptions.

The national council appoints a national court of honour each year to advise the executive board in matters pertaining to merit badges, medals, etc.

The national council elects one member of the national court of honour to act as a chairman (he is called the national scout commissioner) and at least seven others from the same body to act with the chairman as the executive committee of the national court of honour.

The national chaplain is ex-officio a member of the national court of honour.

ADDRESS TO HIERARCHY

The organising council prepared an address to the hierarchy. It set out the advantages of making scouting available to boys and the importance of ensuring that there should be a Catholic scout organisation for Catholic boys. They pointed out that the two scout organisations in the country were unsuitable. The B-P scouts they described as a branch of an English organisation which was non-sectarian in theory but Protestant in practice. Membership of this organisation, they warned, could undermine the faith of Catholic boys. Referring to Fianna Éireann and Clanna Fodhla they wrote: 'there is another danger to our boys in the fact that they may be led to join other organisations that have the semblance of scouting but whose tendencies are political or military. This is a danger that is urgent...'

The organising council indicated to the bishops that the aim of the scout organisation, the draft constitution of which they were forwarding, 'shall be Catholic, first, last and all the time'. The bishops were assured that all who had been approached – members of the clergy and laity, heads of the boys' colleges and schools in and around Dublin, the provincial of the Christian Brothers, members of the St Vincent de Paul Society and of the Catholic Young Men's Society (CYMS) – were 'ardent supporters' of the establishment of a Catholic boy scout organisation. In concluding their appeal to the bishops to approve the setting up of the proposed organisation, the organising council quoted from an address by Pius XI to an international gathering of Catholic scouts in the summer of 1925. In what could be regarded as a charter of Catholic scouting, the Holy Father ended his address: 'You are Catholic scouts. You are scouts who bring to your scouting the beautiful and sublime characteristics of your Catholic Faith and Catholic life. Scouting is a good thing but in itself it is only a good thing of earth. You by your Faith and spiritual motives, doing all for the glory of God, turn it into an affair of heaven.'

APPROVAL OF HIERARCHY

At their autumn meeting in October 1926 the hierarchy approved of the establishment of the CBSI and this was communicated to the organising council in November. However, it was emphasised that before troops could be organised in a diocese the permission of the appropriate bishop would be required. This did not bode well for the future success of the proposed scout association. Many of the bishops and senior clergy had little enthusiasm for the new scout organisation. With Fianna Éireann principally in mind, they were loath to encourage a disciplined organisation in which someone would come between parents and their children. They also considered that the CBSI would be attracting members from existing youth organisations such as youth clubs, papal cadets, CYMS and above all sodalities. These last were well established and flourishing in every diocese and practically every parish. They ensured that the boys and girls and young men and women who joined them attended a monthly evening prayer service and confessed and received Holy Communion once a month.

CHAPTER TWO

The Early Years

BEGINNINGS OF CBSI IN DUBLIN

ARCHBISHOP EDWARD BYRNE conveyed his permission to the organising council in mid-December 1926 to establish troops in his archdiocese. In January 1927 the organising council became the national council of the CBSI and appointed a national executive board. Fr Tom Farrell acted as secretary to both and until a premises became available in 1935 at 71 St Stephen's Green, the apartments of the two Farrells, especially that of Tom's brother Ernest at 87 St Stephen's Green, were the headquarters of the CBSI. This prompted the CBSI heritage group to site a plaque to the memory of the Frs Farrell in the porch of University Church in 2001.

Ernest continued to promote the CBSI energetically. Between 8 March and 25 May he had excerpts from the CBSI *Handbook* published in the front page of *Our Boys*. In the issue of 9 June under 'Scout notes' he described a concert presented by the Visitation troop of Fairview in the Catholic Commercial Club. And from 23 June to 18 August he ensured that the front page of *Our Boys* carried an account of one or other of the CBSI merit badges. In the meantime he had prepared, on behalf of the national council, a pamphlet *How to Organise a Troop* and advertised it in *Our Boys* and elsewhere. Frs Tom and Ernest availed of every opportunity to urge their colleagues to establish troops in their parishes. Ernest addressed deanery meetings of the clergy on the subject, while Tom met the heads of the various religious orders in order to persuade them to set up troops in their churches, colleges and schools.

EARLY ORGANISATION AND ACTIVITIES

From the outset the St Vincent de Paul Society availed of every opportunity to promote the CBSI and many of its members were involved in the establishment of troops throughout the country. The Catholic press, not least the *Irish Catholic* through October 1927, kept the development of the CBSI before the minds of the public. Reports of a meeting of the national council of 21 November 1927 listed its members as: Sir Joseph A. Glynn (president); Fr Tom Farrell, CC (hon sec); Fr Joseph Dwyer, CC; Fr Ernest Farrell, CC; Fr Laurence Sheehan, CC; John O'Neill and Thomas J. Bradley (hon treasurers); Dr Paul Carton; Dr William Cussen; Alfred E. Jones; James J. Pakenham; and Patrick M. Rath. Pakenham and Rath later served as Dublin diocesan and national commissioners respectively. The meeting decided that uniforms and badges should be Irish-made and it was reported that twenty-three troops had started since the previous meeting.

The first meeting of the Dublin diocesan council was held on 23 January 1929 at 87 St Stephen's Green (University Church presbytery). The following officers were elected: Fr Tom Farrell, CC (chairman); Dr J. F. Falvey (vice-chairman); Dr Conor Martin (secretary); Fr T. O'Callaghan, CC (treasurer); James J. Pakenham (commissioner); and Séamus O'Higgins, scoutmaster (merit badge secretary). The first 'Grand March' of the Dublin CBSI was held on 21 April 1929 and it was reviewed by the Chief Scout, John O'Neill.

AFFILIATION OF EARLY TROOPS OF CATHOLIC SCOUTS TO CBSI

Apart from promoting the establishment of new troops the national council concerned itself with affiliating existing Catholic scout troops. One such group was the Visitation troop at Fairview in Dublin. This was set up in 1926. Some of the members, who wore a grey uniform, had been in Fianna Éireann. The troop affiliated with the CBSI at the beginning of 1927 but members not change their grey for the navy-blue uniforms of the CBSI until four years later.

The scout group set up by Fr Ernest Farrell at Greystones was also affiliated. It seems that he considered its members to be the first Irish Catholic boy scouts. In *Our Boys* of 29 April 1926 he recalled that on the previous 30 March he had officiated at the funeral of patrol leader Kevin Brack. He wrote that Kevin was the first to seek admission and be enrolled in the Catholic scouts and was an exemplary leader of his patrol.

FIRST TROOPS

As soon as the CBSI was established Fr Ernest Farrell set up a troop at University Church. It consisted mainly of the altar boys associated with the church. He named it the 1st Dublin. However to ensure the affiliation of the Fairview troop of Catholic scouts to the CBSI he agreed that they retain their title 1st Dublin and the troop of University Church was renamed the 'headquarters troop'. It was intended that it should be a model or demonstration troop, whose meetings could be attended by those who wished to form their own troops. In January 1941 the Fairview troop, the 1st Dublin, successfully applied to the then new archbishop, John Charles McQuaid, to use the extra title 'Archbishop's Own' and to wear his coat of arms.

After his appointment as parish priest of Aughrim Street parish Fr Ernest Farrell set up the 9th Dublin which was titled 'Founder's Own'. In 1949 this expanded and some of its members established the 10th Dublin. Subsequently both these troops were remarkably successful in diocesan and national competitions. In 1998, owing to a decline in membership, they were forced to merge.

Also at the beginning of 1927 the 2nd Dublin troop was established. It was associated with the Carmelite church of St Teresa at Clarendon Street in the city centre. Within a short time the CBSI at Clarendon Street was comprised of six troops. Besides the 2nd Dublin, the group consisted of the 7th, 10th, 14th, 15th and 24th Dublin. In addition, it also had a knights errant clan and a pipers' band. The group's parades, camps, exhibitions, concerts and sports were widely covered in the press. So much so that the group, with a membership of more than 250, came to be referred to simply as the Catholic Boy Scouts of Ireland.

Much of the remarkable success of this troop can be attributed to Joe Carey. A former member of the boys' club associated with St Teresa's, he had been enthused by Fr Farrell's articles in *Our Boys* in 1925 and 1926. In 1926 he and five companions visited Fr Farrell at Greystones and were briefed about his 'scout group'. Fr Farrell promised then that when the CBSI had been sanctioned they would together establish a troop. Unfortunately, after an internal dispute, Joe Carey left the 2nd Dublin in 1929 and with others set up the Catholic Ranger Scouts of Ireland. Members of the group were older than the average age of scouts; they wore a grey uniform and many of them were proficient in first aid. However, after failing to win the sanction of Archbishop Byrne, the group disbanded after a few years.

EARLY YEARS IN BELFAST

In the summer of 1927 numerous scout patrols and groups were formed in the Catholic districts of Belfast. Members had no uniform or distinguishing mark beyond a scout stave. In the autumn, following prompting from the national council of the CBSI, a general meeting was held in a community hall in Sultan Street in St Peter's parish in the city centre. The scouts who attended were organised along the lines of the CBSI and agreement was reached that the basic scout uniform should be a green hat, a green shirt and navy-blue trousers. Two troops were formed: 1st Belfast (associated with the Redemptorist church of the Holy Redeemer at Clonard) and 2nd Belfast (associated with St Peter's parish). The first major event in which the Belfast scouts took part was a church parade to the Redemptorist church at Clonard on Christmas day 1927.

Over 4,000 boys took part in the parade and reports of it made the local clergy aware of the potential for good of this new youth movement. They appealed to members of the St Vincent de Paul Society to help organise it in the city parishes. The original troop attached to Clonard monastery was disbanded as its members were directed to join the new troops in their own parishes. Eventually these new troops were named as follows: 2nd Belfast (St Peter's), 3rd Belfast (St Mary's), 4th Belfast (St Paul's), 5th Belfast (Holy Rosary), 6th Belfast (St Malachy's), 7th Belfast (St Matthew's) and 8th Belfast (St Patrick's). Initially, out of deference to the part played by the original troop associated with the Redemptorist church at Clonard, the title '1st Belfast' was not used. Later it was given to a troop at St John's. At the same time as the establishment of the first eight troops Patrick Hazelton became commissioner of the Belfast Catholic scouts.

Bishop Joseph MacRory followed the development of Catholic scouting in his diocese with great interest. In June 1928 a parade of the Belfast scouts was held in 'Seán's Park' in the Upper Whiterock district, which was used as a Gaelic football ground. The bishop presented each troop with a flag. Subsequently he bought the grounds and they were used as a sports field by the Christian Brothers school. For many years they were also used by the Belfast troops for their annual camp.

In 1931 Fr Patrick McAlea, a curate in Castlewellan, County Down, was planning to establish a troop in his own parish. He met the Frs Farrell in Dublin, who persuaded him to set it up in conjunction with the CBSI. The first investiture of this troop was held in August 1931 and it was the first troop of the CBSI in Northern Ireland. The affiliation of the Belfast troops was precipitated by their desire to take part in the Eucharistic Congress, which was to be held in June 1932. A few months before the congress the Belfast diocesan commissioner, Patrick Hazelton and some Belfast scout chaplains met the CBSI Chief Scout, J. B. Whelehan, and others. Negotiations for the amalgamation of the Belfast scouts with the CBSI were completed in May. As part of this arrangement the Belfast scouts exchanged their green shirt for the navy-blue of the CBSI.

Involvement of the Belfast scouts in the Eucharistic Congress and the national pilgrimage to Rome in 1934 led to a surge of recruits in that year and the number of troops in the city increased from eight to fourteen. And the Knights of St Columbanus donated the Columbanus Shield for which the Belfast troops competed annually from 1935 onwards.

BEGINNINGS IN WATERFORD

Fr (later Canon) Michael C. Crotty was the outstanding promoter of the CBSI in the diocese of Waterford and Lismore. In 1927, while serving as administrator in the cathedral parish he established the 1st and 2nd Waterford troops. The 1st Waterford, known as St Joseph's, was closed because of a lack of support in less than two years. In the autumn of 1928, with the help of the De La Salle brothers, he set up the 3rd Waterford at their school in Stephen's Street. Then in 1930 on being appointed parish priest of Abbeyside, near Dungarvan, he set up the 4th Waterford. Later, in 1933, on becoming parish priest of Cahir, he established the 7th Tipperary. In each parish his procedure was similar. He appealed to members of the local branch of the St Vincent de Paul Society to supply leaders for the proposed troops and to serve on committees to supervise their operation.

Subsequently the CBSI flourished in the diocese of Waterford and Lismore. Among the many fine troops in the diocese the 4th Waterford from Abbeyside was the most highly regarded for its determination to achieve excellence in the various facets of scouting. Time and time again between 1938 and 1976 Abbeyside won the Farrell Cup. This was donated by Waterford solicitor R. J. Farrell and for the most part was competed for annually by most of the troops in the diocese. The troop was also more successful than any other troop in the annual competition for the diocesan shield. Success in this competition meant the troop could represent the diocese at the Melvin trophy competition. From 1949 onwards this was held annually, generally at the National Scout Campsite at Larch Hill. Abbeyside represented Waterford on twelve occasions and were four times winner of the All-Ireland competition. Members of the troop were also in the scout contingents at all national events in which the CBSI took part. For two periods the troop had a pipe band and as part of its golden jubilee celebrations published an admirable record of scouting at Abbeyside.

Over the years the Waterford troops with the highest membership were those under the auspices of the De La Salle Brothers. Because of its popular-

ity the 3rd Waterford was able to set up the 7th Waterford in 1931. A further
De La Salle troop, the 13th Waterford, was founded in 1942. The De La Salle
troops were represented at the CBSI's national events and annually took part
with considerable success in diocesan and national competitions. In the 1940s
and 1950s the De La Salle scout pipe band featured at most local major religious and sporting events. From 1928 to 1995 members of the De La Salle
Congregation acted as leaders of the troops or units. In 1970 the congregation also acquired a training site for the troops at Faithlegg on the outskirts of
the city.

In the 1990s the 3rd and 13th Waterford were remarkably successful in
competitions and in 2000 the 13th Waterford won the Melvin trophy.
Following the restructuring of the scouting organisation, the 3rd, 7th and 13th
Waterford became the Waterford region's De La Salle Scout Group in 2004.

BEGINNINGS IN LIMERICK

The CBSI was established in Limerick following a meeting on the last
Sunday of January 1928. At this meeting in St Munchin's college, chaired by
Fr James Cowper, preparations were made to set up troops in the city
parishes. Eventually these were named as follows: 1st Limerick (St
Michael's), 2nd Limerick (St Mary's), 3rd Limerick (St John's), 4th Limerick
(St Munchin's) and 5th Limerick (St Joseph's). The Limerick scouts publicly
paraded as a body for the first time in August 1928 at the celebrations mark-
ing the 60th anniversary of the Arch-confraternity associated with the
Redemptorists' church in the city. Thereafter they held an annual St
Patrick's Day parade through the city. Limerick scouts provided first-aid and
other services during the Eucharistic Congress of 1932 and some went on
the national pilgrimage to Rome in 1934.

During the 1930s, apart from church parades and other routine exercises, various programmes of activities were devised by the individual troops.
Among these were boating, boxing, first-aid, hurling, gymnastics, pipe
bands and swimming galas. The annual competition for the diocesan shield
was first held in 1935. In 1953 during an address at the celebration of the silver jubilee of the CBSI in Limerick diocese Canon James Cowper outlined
the manner in which Catholic scouting was viewed in Limerick. He noted
that scouting helped the providers of education: the home, the Church and
the school. This it did by filling a boy's spare time with useful work that
looked like play in the healthy environment of good companionship. But,
he pointed out, the ultimate aim of Catholic scouting was to turn out
young men of sterling character and high integrity, where religion was not

just a matter of Sunday observance but rather a manner of life in which they would not forget that they were 'first and last and all the time Catholics'. Canon James Cowper (diocesan chaplain) spent a lifetime promoting the CBSI in Limerick, as did John C. Duggan (diocesan commissioner) and Kevin B. Dineen (district scoutmaster).

EARLY YEARS IN CORK

In the pamphlet *The First Few years of CBSI in Cork* Jack Lee recollected the beginnings in Cork as follows:

> CBSI in Cork started in a room in the South Terrace in 1930. My own introduction to the movement came about by a chance meeting with a friend of mine, Alfred Byford, who lived in the same locality as myself (Albert Road).
>
> On the evening of Saturday 12 July 1930 I was returning home after doing some errand for my mother and my route took me through South Terrace. There on the steps of one of its large Georgian houses I noticed this chap Byford wearing a boy scout uniform. My curiosity aroused, I approached him and asked him about the uniform and what it was all about. When he informed me that he was a member of the new troop of Catholic Boy Scouts of Ireland just being formed I immediately expressed my wish to join. We then entered the house together and my friend led me into a room on the right-hand side of the hall.
>
> There were about twenty-five lads in the room ranging in age from twelve to fifteen and six young men who obviously were scoutmasters. A few of the boys were dressed in part uniform. There was a wonderful air of excitement and enthusiasm and a feeling of great comradeship. After my friend had introduced me to one of the scoutmasters, P .J. Sheehan, the latter took my name and other particulars and told me to join one of the groups who were just then starting on their rawly tests.
>
> I went from group to group taking in eagerly all that was going on. During the meeting a consignment of uniforms arrived, and much to their delight most of the boys left the room that night with a complete uniform, including a timber pole called a stave.
>
> Before we dismissed that night Mr Sheehan informed us that we would be attending an instruction parade the following day and he instructed us to meet at Douglas fingerpost at 3 o'clock.
>
> Scoutmasters present at that meeting on 12 July 1930 were:
>
> P. J. Sheehan, C. J. O'Hanlon, B. G. Burkley, D. Lehane, A Foley, and D. O'Connell.

Following the establishment of the CBSI Fr Tom Farrell on behalf of the national council had appealed to the clergy in Cork as elsewhere to set up troops in their parishes. A similar appeal was also made to the Cork members of the Knights of St Columbanus to help to this end. However, it was not until scouts had been seen on parade at the ceremonies to mark the centenary of Catholic Emancipation in June 1929 that steps were taken to set up the CBSI in the diocese of Cork.

In the autumn Bishop Daniel Cohalan sanctioned the establishment of the CBSI in his diocese. At the beginning of 1930 a diocesan council was set up with Fr William Johnson as honorary secretary. Some members of the Knights of St Columbanus came forward to act as leaders and made their meeting place at 30 South Terrace available for the establishment of a 'training troop'. By 12 July 1930, when Jack Lee joined this troop, the diocesan council had decided that the troop should mount a guard of honour at a liturgical reception for the new papal nuncio, Monsignor Pascal Robinson, OFM. This was to be held at the Cathedral of St Mary and St Anne on 15 July.

The national council was anxious that the first public outing of the Cork scouts would be a success. Knight Errant Lorcan O'Higgins was despatched to drill and inspect the uniforms of the 'training troop' at Douglas national school on the Sunday prior to the liturgical reception. Then on the evening of the function John Fitzmaurice arrived. His role, it seems, was to help plan the details of the parade. Fitzmaurice had served as scoutmaster of the 1st Dublin troop at Fairview. After a number of troops were set up in the city, he became district scoutmaster. In the late 1930s he conducted training courses for Dublin scouts. Highly regarded by his peers, he was also a brother of Colonel James Fitzmaurice of the Irish Air Corps who took part in the historic first successful east-west transatlantic flight in 1928. In the event the Cork scouts acquitted themselves very well at the reception for the papal nuncio and on the following day at a garden party in his honour in the grounds of University College, Cork.

In September 1930 the Diocesan Council directed that the members of the 'training troop' should be distributed into six parish troops. Thereby the following core troops of the Cork scouts were formed as follows: 1st Cork (Cathedral), 2nd Cork (South Parish), 3rd Cork (St Patrick's), 4th Cork (Sts Peter and Paul's), 5th Cork (The Lough) and 6th Cork (St Columba's, Douglas).

Throughout 1931 membership of the Cork troops increased rapidly. Their weekly meetings, monthly church parades and weekend hikes were well attended. In May all the troops were inspected by Professor J. B. Whelehan, the Chief Scout, at a rally in the grounds of UCC. In July the city troops and some from the county held a diocesan camp on the demesne of the ruined Kilbrittain Castle, County Cork. Bishop Cohalan spent a day at the camp and expressed his satisfaction with the manner in which the organisation was developing in the diocese. In September Dominic O'Hanlon was appointed diocesan scout commissioner. He had been a B-P scoutmaster when residing in the Channel Islands. Also in September the first steps were taken to erect a headquarters for the Cork scouts at Summerhill. This was known as 'the Hut' and was to serve in this role until 1963. In May 1932 the Cork scouts held a rally in connection with an Irish industrial fair. Among others the Chief Scout, Bishop Cohalan and Lord Mayor Seán French were on the reviewing stand.

The Cork scouts were to become one of the most vibrant branches of the CBSI. Among its outstanding leaders were Walter J. McGrath and Con Twomey, a member of the 1st Larch Hill Training Team. McGrath, a distinguished journalist with the *Cork Examiner* and *Evening Echo*, served at both diocesan and national level. In March 1950 he visited the B-P training centre at Gilwell Park, London, and was briefed on the 'bob-a-job' scheme. He supervised a successful trial of the scheme by the Cork scouts during the following Easter week. Thereafter it became a part of the annual programme of the CBSI and from 1961 onwards became a major source of funding for the association. He published *Fifty Years a-Growing: Pictorial History of the Catholic Boy Scouts of Ireland* in 1979.

CHANGES IN UNIFORM AND SCOUT GRADES

From the outset the uniform of the CBSI was a navy-blue, short-sleeved shirt and navy shorts, grey stockings, black shoes and wide-brimmed scout hat. In the early years many troops also had their members carry a five-foot stave. The badge of the new association, the green shamrock and the red Greek cross, was on the left breast pocket of the uniform. Initially the Fairview troop wore a grey shirt and even after joining the CBSI continued to do so until 1939. Ironically, in 1952 the CBSI in Dublin diocese and much of the rest of the country switched from the blue to a grey shirt.

In the early years senior leaders wore a navy Norfolk jacket over their scout shirt with navy breeches, navy puttees and black boots. The breeches and puttees were soon replaced by navy slacks. In the mid-1960s leaders' uniforms included charcoal grey slacks as an alternative to navy shorts. In the early 1950s the broad-brimmed hat was replaced by a Glengarry type beret. In 1969 a bright-blue long-sleeved shirt and navy slacks were introduced with a black beret. In 1972, owing to its identification with volunteers of the Provisional IRA, the black beret had to be replaced with a light blue one. In 1971 a red anorak-type waterproof jacket was introduced as an official outer garment. However, it did not prove to be popular and quickly fell into disuse.

From the beginning the association used differently coloured enamelled cap badges to indicate rank. This was discontinued after 1979. The rank badges of scoutmasters (scout leaders, scouters, unit leaders), commissioners and other leaders were changed from time to time but since the 1980s have been effectively standardised. Cub scouts/*Macaoimh* were introduced in 1934 and their uniform has not changed. It remains the cap, jersey and shorts, though since 1973 slacks have also been optional for cubs. In 1969 the change from Knights errant to Venturers also involved some slight variations in the new uniform. Between 1963 and 1966 among Dublin scouts there was a development known as the 'Senior Scout experiment' which attempted to promote a programme suitable for scouts from fifteen to seventeen years old. This section used a distinctive uniform with a maroon beret and maroon epaulettes on the shirt.

From the outset the CBSI had six grades of scout: rawly, second class, first class, star, national and silver palms. These continued up to the end of the 1960s. Since then the new grades are invested scout, proficient scout, star and national, the highest grade being the holder of the Chief Scout's award. All the grades had their appropriate tests.

In the CBSI there were variations from time to time in the number and kinds of tests required to be taken at each grade. But, for the most part, there were ten tests to qualify as a rawly scout, fourteen more to be passed for qualification as a second class scout and success in a further eighteen was required to become a first class scout. The star scout, in addition, would hold between ten and fifteen merit badges for proficiency in different skills. Finally the national scout would have seven more merit badges and some further reason for reaching that status. The silver palm was generally presented to those who had given a life-time of service to the association. The tests were conducted by a body independent of the troop whose members were taking them. Very often they were supervised by representatives of a neighbouring troop.

The second class scout was entitled to have a sheath knife. But this was to be worn only with full uniform or at camp. From the mid-1960s onwards, as the possibility of violence became stronger in society, there was an increasing tendency for scouts not to have or use knives except at their annual camps.

The matter of indiscipline or misconduct was first brought before a court of honour, made up of representatives of the patrol. Later, if a resolution had not been found, it came before the troop's court of honour, on which the chaplain and scout leader would be represented. Occasionally a diocesan court of honour was established to deal with cases of grave misconduct.

CHIEF SCOUTS, CENTENARY OF CATHOLIC EMANCIPATION

At a meeting of the National Executive of CBSI in January 1927 Board John O'Neill was elected Chief Scout. A resident of Greystones, he had been associated with Fr Ernest Farrell's early 'scout group'. He had been a member of Seanad Éireann from March to September 1925 and was one of the Knights of St Columbanus who signed the petition to the hierarchy to sanction the establishment of the CBSI. An importer and assembler of cars, his business failed at the end of the 1920s and he was in serious financial difficulties. For this reason Fr Tom Farrell and other members of the national executive board were relieved when he resigned from his position as Chief Scout towards the end of 1930.

The highlight of the ceremonies to mark the centenary of Catholic Emancipation was a High Mass held on 23 June 1929 in the Phoenix Park, Dublin. It was attended by dignitaries of Church and State. The CBSI eagerly grasped the opportunity to help with the organisation of the event, which most of them were mustered to attend. Just under 2,000 scouts camped in the Phoenix Park for a few days prior to the special High Mass. On the morning of the national celebration they held their own Mass in the grounds of the Royal Hibernian School and during the High Mass many of them acted as stewards, water-carriers and manned first-aid centres.

Unlike his brother Ernest, Fr Tom Farrell had little first-hand experience of basic scouting. So to acquire a grasp on the practicalities of scouting and leadership, he went on a training course at Gilwell Park in London during his annual holidays in 1929. He had a pleasant and outgoing personality, moved easily in all circles and wherever he went was the object of much affection. A scout at heart, he treasured the time he spent at Gilwell Park and the picture of his smiling face over his name and I.F.S. (Irish Free State) can be seen at Gilwell Park with those of many other distinguished visitors to the training centre.

The first official CBSI pilgrimage to Lourdes was held in September

1930. The party included John O'Neill, the Chief Scout, Joseph B. Whelehan, future Chief Scout, Frs Ernest and Tom Farrell, five diocesan commissioners and about 200 scouts of various ranks. The decorum of the scouts at ceremonies and their general conduct aroused much favourable comment. Fr Tom Farrell availed of the opportunity the pilgrimage offered to become closely acquainted with many of the scout leaders.

Towards the end of January 1931 the national executive board elected Professor Joseph B Whelehan, MA, of Stradbrook Hall, Blackrock, to the position of Chief Scout. He was born in 1882 at Tyrellspass, County Westmeath and was educated at the local national school. In his teens he became a member of the Irish Christian Brothers, spent several years teaching and for a period was a novice master. After leaving the order he secured an appointment at St Jarlath's College, Tuam, in 1917 and for a number of years he was dean of studies there. At St Jarlath's he acquired the then customary but honorary title of 'Professor' which although he resigned from teaching in 1922, he retained for the rest of his life.

An ardent member of Sinn Féin, he was returned to the Second Dáil for County Galway in 1921. He supported the Anglo-Irish Treaty and during the heated debate on the treaty in December 1921 was most active in attempting to facilitate a *rapprochement* between the opposing sides. A confidant of President William T. Cosgrave, from 1923 to 1927 he served as an assistant to a succession of ministers for industry and commerce in the first three Irish Free State governments. In 1927 he was appointed comptroller of the stationery office, in which post he served until 1949.

When in 1927 he withdrew from political life Whelehan became involved in promoting clubs for young people. Thus the two Frs Farrell had little difficulty in persuading him to help with the organisation and development of the CBSI. He became a member of the national executive Board and in that capacity he had accompanied the first official CBSI pilgrimage to Lourdes in September 1930. From 1937 onwards he was a member of the committee set up to oversee the care of Larch Hill, the CBSI's national campsite. From 1931 to 1961 he was re-elected each year to the post of Chief Scout. A man of deep religious conviction, he was far more interested in the spiritual side of scouting then in the mechanics of the development and expansion of the association. He died on 31 October 1968.

CHAPTER THREE

Era of Fr Tom Farrell

FR TOM FARRELL ON THE CATHOLIC SCOUT MOVEMENT

In *The Irish Monthly* of February 1932 Fr Tom Farrell set out the aim of Catholic scouting as follows:

> To cultivate, train, develop and strengthen all the faculties – physical, intellectual, moral, religious – which contribute in the boy's nature and human dignity and to do so with the high object of helping him to discharge efficiently and faithfully his life work for God and man ...From the physical aspect, Catholic scouting endeavours by means of certain play activities, participated in for the most part out of doors, to build up for the boy a sound, healthy body. From the intellectual point of view, it strives to create in him a healthy mind and to store it with knowledge beneficial to himself and useful to others. From the moral aspect, it endeavours to instil into the boy chivalrous sentiments to keep alive the flame of heroism in his heart and encourage him to cultivate natural and civic virtues. But Catholic scouting demands that there be in his training a deeply religious foundation on which to build. It emphasises the fact that the appeal to natural motives accomplishes little, unaided by divine grace, and so it leads the boy in a practical and cheerful way to make use of prayer and the Sacraments as a means to obtain this divine assistance...

He then illustrated how this aim of Catholic scouting was achieved through adhering to the scout principles, scout promise, scout law, 'the good turn' and practical training in all the branches of scout craft. Ultimately the aim of Catholic scouting, he emphasised, was the building of character. He concluded by praising those who undertook responsibility for troops and reminded them that the spirit of the Catholic scout movement 'is a spirit of service to others, service to the boy, the whole boy, soul and body for God's greater glory'.

EUCHARISTIC CONGRESS, 1932

A Eucharistic Congress was held in Dublin on 22–26 June 1932 to celebrate the fifteen-hundredth anniversary of St Patrick's mission to Ireland. Thousands of people arrived in a festive Dublin for the occasion. The congress was formally opened at St Mary's Pro-Cathedral by Cardinal Lorenso Lauri, the papal legate, in the presence of nine cardinals, more than a hundred bishops and a thousand priests and other religious. An altar was erected on O'Connell Bridge, where the cardinal legate imparted Benediction.

The main events of the Congress were

> *Wednesday 22 June:* Following Exposition of Blessed Sacrament, midnight Mass was celebrated at every church in Dublin.
>
> *Thursday 23 June:* 'Men's Day' – more than 250,000 men attended Mass in the Phoenix Park.
>
> *Friday 24 June:* 'Ladies Day' – some 200,000 women attended Mass in the Phoenix Park.
>
> *Saturday 25 June:* 'Children's Day' – 100,000 children sang 'Missa de Angelis' at a special children's Mass in the Phoenix Park.
>
> *Sunday 26 June:* An estimated million people attended Pontifical High Mass in the Phoenix Park during which John McCormack sang 'Panis Angelicus' and the apostolic blessing of Pius XI was broadcast to the huge congregation.

INVOLVEMENT OF CBSI

When it was announced that the Eucharistic Congress was to be held in Dublin Fr Tom Farrell offered the services of the CBSI to the congress organisers. All troops in Dublin and elsewhere were mustered to take part in it. For the troops from the provinces who would be participating in the week's events, a camp was set up in the grounds of the Carmelite College at Terenure, where 1,500 scouts were accommodated. At the congress the scouts were involved in every kind of duty: water-carrying, traffic-control, providing guards of honour and stewarding. Their most valued contribution was in providing first-aid at major events. In preparation for the congress first-aid squads had been trained in many parts of the country. During the congress these and the Dublin-based units were under the direction of Dr Conor Martin, the CBSI's National Commissioner. The number of scouts who helped with the Congress was impressive. On the final day, Sunday, 26 June, 300 scouts were rostered for the enclosure in the Phoenix

Park at 9 a.m., another 500 as water carriers, 1,200 as stewards; 500 at O'Connell Bridge at 2 p.m. and 200 to take charge of cushions on which the bishops knelt during the Benediction of the Blessed Sacrament. In addition first-aid scouts were assigned to all the railway stations and thirteen other centres as well as along the processional routes.

MAJOR BOOST FOR CBSI

By the end of 1930 the CBSI was firmly established in the four provinces and in nearly every parish in Belfast, Cork, Dublin and Limerick. Troops had also been set up in the diocese of Elphin (at Sligo), Ferns (at Wexford) and Waterford and Lismore (at Waterford and Abbeyside). The Eucharistic Congress provided a major boost to the development of the association. During the months in which troops were preparing to participate in the congress, CBSI leaders at all levels were able to insist on a significant improvement in organisation, training, levels of discipline and attention to detail in the wearing of the uniform. At the congress tens of thousands for the first time saw the 'new scouts' and were impressed by their smart appearance and general deportment. The scouts were featured prominently in the newspapers' extensive pictorial coverage of the major events. Members of the younger clergy, who had responsibility for young people, became particularly interested in the 'new youth movement'. Thus, during the two years following the congress, many new troops were set up and the membership of the CBSI almost doubled. However, within a further few years most of these lapsed, owing mainly to a lack of proper organisation and devoted leadership at local level. And, at the prospect of greater appreciation and use of their skills, many of the scouts who were most proficient in first-aid later joined the Irish Red Cross after it was established in 1939.

PILGRIMAGE TO ROME, 1934

Pius XI proclaimed 1934 to be a Holy Year. This prompted the CBSI to organise a pilgrimage to Rome and Joseph Cardinal MacRory, Archbishop of Armagh, accepted an invitation to lead it. More than 2,000 people joined the pilgrimage, 600 of them members of the CBSI. The luxury liner, SS *Lancastria*, was chartered to convey the pilgrims to Rome.

On 7 March the SS *Lancastria* sailed to Gibraltar. On 11 March it docked in Naples, whence the pilgrims travelled to Rome. The highlight of the pilgrimage was an audience with Pius XI. He spoke in English of the ties between Ireland and the Vatican, praised scouting and blessed the flags of the various troops. On the return journey the pilgrims called to Ceuta, an area of Morocco owned by Spain, on 20 March. A film of the pilgrimage by Movietone News was subsequently shown in Irish cinemas throughout the country.

MELVIN TROPHY

The pilgrimage to Rome was regarded in CBSI circles as a landmark event. Some of the scouts who took part were subsequently numbered among the association's longest-serving and most highly-regarded leaders. Typical was Patrick Hogan (later brigadier general and GOC, Curragh Command), who was to serve as Chief Scout from 1970 to 1974. Among the scouts who distinguished themselves in other ways were Liam Cosgrave, who later became Taoiseach, and Cornelius Ryan, best known for his novels *The Longest day* and *A Bridge too Far*. The CBSI's most coveted trophy is associated with the pilgrimage. Sir Martin Melvin was also one of the pilgrims. Proprietor of *The Universe*, the English Catholic newspaper, he had taken a keen interest from the outset in the development of the CBSI. He had decided to present a valuable trophy to the CBSI for inter-troop competition and had commissioned one of the leading silversmiths of the time, Mia Cranwell, to produce it. In a ceremony on board the *SS Lancastria* on the way to Rome, he formally presented the trophy to the Chief Scout.

The annual All-Ireland inter-diocesan troop competition (one patrol) for the trophy did not begin until August 1949. The trophy was won by the 26th Dublin (Iona Road). The presentation was held on the following Easter Sunday in the grounds of Marlboro' Street schools in the presence of Church and State dignitaries, including the Taoiseach, John A. Costello, and minister for education, Richard Mulcahy. Sir Martin Melvin travelled from Manchester to present the trophy in person. Over one thousand Dublin scouts attended the ceremony. Thereafter the trophy was awarded annually to the winners of the national patrol camp-craft competition until 2003. In 2005 the competition for the Melvin trophy was replaced by the Phoenix Challenge, the winners of which were presented with the statuette of a phoenix which was commissioned by the SI association.

SS LANCASTRIA

The pilgrims, especially the scouts, forged close links of friendship with members of the crew and staff of the *Lancastria* during their seventeen-day cruise. Subsequently they were greatly saddened by the fate of the luxury liner. At the beginning of World War II she was commandeered by the British government and refitted for war service. In 1940 after helping to evacuate British forces from Norway, the ship was directed to St Nazaire in France to evacuate soldiers of the British Expeditionary Force and RAF personnel. On 17 June 1940 the HMT *Lancastria* was bombed, and in less than twenty minutes sank with the loss of 5,000 of the 7,500 on board. To ensure that British morale was not affected by the disaster, Prime Minister Winston Churchill directed that news of it was not to be published until after the war.

After World War II the *Lancastria* Association was set up to cherish the memory of those lost on the ship. The association erected a memorial in St Katherine Cree church in Leadenhall Street, London. Over the years memories of the *HMT Lancastria* and its crew remained fresh in the minds of many members of the CBSI and they harboured the wish to erect a memorial to those who had perished when the ship was sunk. Eventually Scouting Ireland decided to erect an appropriate memorial at Larch Hill, partly to honour those lost in the ship and partly to celebrate the unification of the SAI and the CBSI. In August 2004 the memorial, an anchor, was formally unveiled and blessed before a large representative gathering of scouts and members of the *Lancastria* Association.

LARCH HILL

A second official pilgrimage to Lourdes took place in 1936. In that year also the national executive board and Chief Scout appealed to all members of the Irish hierarchy to promote the CBSI in their dioceses. They set out the merits of Catholic scouting and warned that 'Catholic youth are being drawn into organisations which are neither Catholic in principle nor Irish in origin'. They pointed out that detailed instruction as to the establishment of a troop and courses of instruction for chaplains and officers were then available.

In 1937–8 the national executive board, by then meeting every month except July and August, was preoccupied with the need for a national campsite. At the time two properties which seemed to be suitable became available. One was part of Santry Park, north of Dublin city. In 1937 a very successful Dublin diocesan camp had been held there, with diocesan commissioner William T. Kinsella acting as camp chief. As a result, members of the national executive board were largely in favour of acquiring it.

The other property was an estate of eighty-eight acres called Larch Hill. It was situated in Tibradden in the foothills of the Dublin mountains not far from the border with County Wicklow. Larch Hill house, on the estate, had been built prior to 1835 for John O'Neill, a wealthy Dublin merchant, whose city residence was in Fitzwilliam Square. It was subsequently occupied by Courtney Kenny Clarke until 1873. In 1912 it became a hospice for sick children and the house and ancillary buildings were used as a convalescent home for British soldiers during World War I. After being occupied by a succession of private owners, by the late 1930s the buildings and the estate were in a very poor condition. But Professor Whelehan, the Chief Scout, argued, in the event correctly, that while housing development would eventually overrun Santry this was not very likely in the case of Larch Hill. He succeeded in persuading the national executive board to purchase it. The CBSI was able to do this by virtue of the profits which the association made on the fares of the non-scout pilgrims to Rome in 1934 – which amounted to £3,000 – as well as making use of a donation of £500 from the Knights of St Columbanus.

The formal opening of Larch Hill was held on Whit Sunday, 4 June 1938. In a memorable ceremony, in which over 400 scouts from Dublin and other troops participated, the central event was an outdoor Mass, described in the press as 'the first outdoor Mass in the Dublin mountains since the Penal Laws'. It was celebrated by Fr Leo McCann. He was typical of a number of Dublin priests then active in promoting the CBSI. As well as periods spent as chaplain to troops in parishes at Fairview and Iona Road, he held several national headquarters' posts including director of knights errant, the senior section of the CBSI; director of publicity; and director of education. Thirty years later when he was parish priest of Sallynoggin and chaplain to the parish troop, he returned to Larch Hill to celebrate Mass marking the 30th anniversary of its formal opening.

PUBLICATIONS

From the outset publications were produced at local and diocesan level from within the ranks of the CBSI but most were short-lived. *Scouthood*, a newsletter for adult leaders, was issued monthly in the early 1930s, and diocesan scout newsletters were used to disseminate directions from the national executive board and the Chief Scout. The most important publication was *The Catholic Scout*, a popular monthly magazine. It played a significant role in spreading and popularising the CBSI. Appearing twelve times a year from 1932 to 1939, it was terminated because of to war-time restrictions. It contained a selection of boys' stories, articles and scout news and was edited by Commissioner Ernest Cullen.

From 1942 onwards Fr Leo McCann acted as director of publicity for the CBSI and ensured that scout functions were covered in a 'Scout Notes' column in the Saturday issue of the *Evening Herald*, regular reports by 'William the Scout' in *Our Boys*, articles in *CYMS Review* and the *Standard* and occasional insertions in the national press. In 1943, 1944 and 1945 *The Catholic Scout Leaders' Bulletin* was published monthly. Apart from routine reports it carried articles on various aspects of scouting by scout leaders from around the country.

By the end of 1944 the publicity department had published the following booklets: *The Catholic Scout Movement* (Fr Tom Farrell's article in *The Irish Monthly* of February 1932), *Scouting for Catholics, Investiture Ceremonial, Handbook of Organisation and Rules, Troop Committee Work, Letters to a New Scoutmaster, How to Run a Troop, A Think in Time, Why be a Boy Scout? Is your Son a Scout?* and *Boy Scout's Camp Book*.

ARCHBISHOP JOHN C. MCQUAID'S FIRST CONTACT WITH CBSI

Reverend Dr John C. McQuaid, who was dean of studies (1928–31) and president (1931–39) of Blackrock College, became archbishop of Dublin at the end of 1940. He was to become noted, among other things, for his interest in education and the wellbeing of the poor and young people. In January 1941, in his first formal contact with the CBSI as archbishop, he granted permission to the 1st Dublin troop to be known as the 'Archbishop's Own' to wear his coat of arms. In April he requested a report on the state of scouting in the archdiocese from Rev Dr Charles F. Hurley, diocesan scout chaplain. Dr Hurley reported that there was a troop of scouts in thirty-four of the eighty-four parishes of the archdiocese, that there were two each in the parishes of Donnybrook and Dún Laoghaire and that there were three troops associated with the Dominican church in Dominick Street and two with the Carmelite church in Clarendon Street.

The archbishop did not consider that Dr Hurley was active enough in promoting the spread of the CBSI and in May appointed Fr Dan Gallagher to succeed him. Fr Gallagher did not disappoint. Within weeks he circularised parishes which did not have a troop of scouts, indicating the archbishop's wish that as many parishes as possible should have a unit, urging those whose troops had lapsed to attempt to reconstitute them and offering whatever help was required to set up or reconstitute troops. In the event, because many city and town parishes already had troops, the attempt to increase the number was not very successful.

DEATH OF FR TOM FARRELL

Fr Tom Farrell, then parish priest of Dolphin's Barn, died suddenly on 12 August 1940. He was deeply and widely mourned especially among the ranks of the CBSI; he had been national secretary of the organisation since 1927. he was succeeded by Tom McHugh, who served for the next seven years. The association commissioned a handsome sculpture and plaque in honour of Fr Farrell, which was unveiled by Archbishop John C. McQuaid in the boardroom of their national headquarters at 71 St Stephen's Green in October 1944. This sculpture by Albert Power was re-erected in the new headquarters at 19 Herbert Place in 1962. Since 2000 installed in the Millennium Room of the national office of Scouting Ireland, it reads:

> *bí ullamh*
> in grateful memory of
> Very Rev T. J. Farrell, P.P., Co-founder
> of the Catholic Boy Scouts of
> Ireland and First National Secretary
> Father Tom died 12th August 1940

Although the plaque implied that he was CBSI's co-founder along with his brother Fr Ernest, members of the association have from the outset regarded him as its founder. For more than two decades the Dublin scouts celebrated an anniversary Mass for Fr Tom. This was held each August either in the Pro-Cathedral or the church of the Holy Cross at Clonliffe College. At the conclusion of the Mass the Chief Scout and invited dignitaries would stand on the steps of the Pro-Cathedral or those of the church of the Holy Cross and take the salute at a march past of the scouts. For a few years the Dublin scouts also marched to Glasnevin cemetery and paid their respects at the grave of Fr Farrell. In addition, they continued one of Fr Tom's cherished initiatives – namely a retreat each summer for scout leaders, sometimes in the Pro-Cathedral or sometimes at the Dominican Retreat Centre at Tallaght.

CHAPTER FOUR

World War II and Thereafter

WORLD WAR II

WITH THE OUTBREAK OF WAR in September 1939 the government declared a state of emergency which was to last until August 1946. Various voluntary defence services were established. The Chief Scout indicated to the authorities the willingness of the CBSI to assist with these. He called leaders of the association to a meeting and directed them to encourage senior scouts to join the emergency services. From the outset the CBSI provided numerous volunteers for the Air Raid Protection (ARP) service. Many members were involved in the distribution of gas masks and instructions in their use.

Already the CBSI had trained and placed on standby first-aid squads. This was supervised by the first sid section of the association. Established in 1934, the section had organised weekly lectures for its members and they had acquired practical experience at events such as carnivals, boxing-matches, rugby matches. In 1939, with war looming, they were instructed with the army in the fall-out from gas warfare. After the Irish Red Cross was established the first aid section marched to the new organisation's depot at Mespil Road and joined as a unit. Because of the training and experience of its members, it became the headquarters division. At the end of the emergency it disaffiliated from the Irish Red Cross. However, by that time many members had formally joined that organisation.

In December 1941 the government decided to establish a junior division of the Local Security Force (LSF). Gerald Boland, the minister for justice, appointed General W.R.E. Murphy to organise it. General Murphy did so with the enthusiastic support of the Chief Scout and Archbishop McQuaid, both of whom he met in connection with it. Subsequently the Dublin section of the CBSI provided hundreds of senior scouts and knights errant to act as leaders in this scheme, which involved the surveillance of strategic facilities.

1940–55

During most of this period Fr Dan Gallagher, Dublin diocesan chaplain, attempted, with the strong support of the archbishop, to increase the number of troops and their membership in the archdiocese. However, he had very limited success. Fr Gallagher's greatest challenge was a lack of leaders. Almost all the sea scout leaders in the troops at Cork, Dublin, Limerick and Waterford joined the naval service. Hundreds of other leaders and senior scouts joined other branches of the defence forces. After the war many of those did not return to their troops. During the Emergency there was rationing of food and fuel, and severe limitations on transport and conditions continued to be stringent for some years. During this period also the average attendance at the annual meetings of the national council was thirty-five, almost a tenth of what it should have been. In the post-war years much dissatisfaction was expressed at the non-affiliation of the association to the World Scout Conference, Scouting's international core.

Throughout the history of the CBSI the Dublin diocesan membership generally represented just under a half of the number of troops and membership of the association nationwide. A review of the annual reports submitted by Fr Gallagher, Dublin diocesan chaplain, and his successor, Fr Morgan Crowe, to Archbishop McQuaid provides an insight at troop level into the strength of the association at this time. The report for 1940–1 listed forty-four troops. In 1945 there were fifty-eight troops with a total membership of 1,883. This was made up of 1,620 scouts (including knights errant, sea scouts and Macaoimh), 109 leaders (scoutmasters and assistant scoutmasters), 107 committee men and 49 chaplains. In 1950 the registered strength in forty-five units was stated to be: chaplains thirty-four, committee men ninety-three, leaders 123, scouts (1,090 (in forty troops), Macaoimh 306 (in eighteen Macaomh Gasraí [cub scout packs]), knights errant sixty-six (in seven Clans) and sea scouts sixty (in five ships). The 1953 report stated simply that there were 'about 1,200 registered scouts in the diocese from thirty-six troops'. In his annual report for 1947 Fr Gallagher stated that the registered strength was: chaplains thirty-nine, committee members 106, leaders (scoutmasters and assistants) 118 and scouts (including knights errant, sea scouts and Macaoimh) 1,361. But he added this cautionary note: 'This figure does not represent the actual strength. The diocesan commissioner records an attendance of 1,800 at the 'Scout Week' parade, which would indicate an actual strength of between 1,850 and 1,900'. Thus it would seem that, generally speaking, the actual number of scouts was 50 per cent greater than the registered number.

Fr Gallagher's reports did not refer to the routine activities of troops in their own parishes. These would involve, apart from the weekly meeting, weekend hikes and camps, monthly church parades, an annual camp and participation in religious ceremonies. Among such ceremonies would be the parish St Patrick's day parade and *Corpus Christi* processions, the diocesan youth Mass and occasional pilgrimages to the Shrine of Blessed Oliver Plunkett at Drogheda or the Shrine of Our Lady at Knock. Some troops also helped to run youth clubs. As a unit the Dublin scouts held three major parades annually. On St Patrick's Day they paraded from the Pro-Cathedral to their headquarters at 71 St Stephen's Green where the Chief Scout took the salute. Each August, after a Memorial Mass for Fr Tom Farrell at Holy Cross College, Clonliffe, about 1,300 scouts were reviewed by the Chief Scout. Until 1943 each spring a 'birthday parade', involving similar numbers, was held from scout headquarters to the Pro-Cathedral for a thanksgiving service. From 1944 onwards this was absorbed into a similar parade to mark the beginning of an annual scout retreat at the Pro-Cathedral. The Dublin scouts also held an annual indoor rally at either the Gaiety Theatre or the Archbishop Byrne Hall at Harrington Street. Troops competed for the Diocesan Shield at Larch Hill and at an annual Sports Day at Blackrock College. In addition, there were monthly conferences of chaplains and of scoutmasters.

From 1947 onwards an annual 'scout week' and an annual regatta and swimming gala, both of which had been interrupted by the war, were resumed. The annual regatta was not well supported, as the number of sea scouts was never significant. The number of air scouts was even less so, with for a short period just one troop at Weston aerodrome near Leixlip, County Kildare. In 1947 also an inter-troop boxing competition was initiated and the Dublin scouts began to help with stewarding at All-Ireland football and hurling matches at Croke Park and at rugby internationals at Lansdowne Road. In 1949 they assisted at the national jubilee celebrations of the Pioneer Total Abstinence Association and, at the express request of the Chief Scout, took part in the National Protest Meeting against Partition. From 1950 onwards a group of fifty, composed of knights errant and senior scouts under the leadership of Diocesan Commissioner William Kinsella, acted as Brancardiers with the annual diocesan pilgrimage to Lourdes. In 1953, 200 Dublin scouts took part in the An Tóstal Parade; the diocesan chaplain in his report of that year stated rather immodestly that 'they were the most colourful part of it'.

Fr Gallagher's reports and correspondence indicate that at that time he and Archbishop McQuaid had three major concerns. The first was the need to establish the CBSI across the archdiocese. They were successful in ensuring that the number of parish troops increased slightly. They also attempted to have troops established in association with the colleges and boys' secondary schools in the greater Dublin area. Despite the archbishop's strong support for this, only three such troops were established: in Blackrock College in 1939, for which he as president had been mainly responsible, in St Mary's College, Rathmines, in 1941 and in Synge Street CBS in 1945. The archbishop considered that troops in the colleges and secondary schools would be ideal for developing leaders and was gravely disappointed at the unwillingness of the college and school authorities to have troops attached to their institutions.

Their second concern was to provide sufficient numbers of suitable and trained leaders. Fr Gallagher proposed that a 'cadet troop' be set up for this purpose. But this was rejected by a conference of scoutmasters.

Their third concern was the need for adequate religious training for scouts in general and scout leaders in particular. From 1948 onwards provision was made for integrating a Catholic element into training courses. There is a reference to this in the diocesan chaplain's report for 1949:

> A comprehensive training course was carried through during the year. It consisted of (1) a specified course of scout reading, with special reference to the *Handbook, Constitution and rules of CBSI* and other publications stressing the Catholic aspect of scouting. (2) A series of lectures delivered in the spring. The lectures were on practical scouting subjects, but the series concluded with a talk on the Catholic-Action aspect of scout leadership. (3) A testing out, under camping conditions, of the knowledge imparted in the lectures. (4) Practice in leadership. The trainees were posted to various scout troops to undertake leadership for a period under the observation of the training committee. (5) A written test, the questions being based on the prescribed course of reading.

In 1953, twenty-five senior scouts were formed into a new and separate 'cadet' troop. In addition to their own course they attended the following lectures which had been provided for all scout leaders:

'Palestine in lantern slides' by Monsignor Patrick Boylan VG.
'Problems of adolescence' by Rev Professor E.F. O'Doherty, UCD.
'Church versus communism', by Rev Professor G. Mitchell, St Patrick's

College, Maynooth.
'Leadership', by Rev Professor E.F. O'Doherty, UCD.
'The weather', by John Byrne, meteorologist, Collinstown.
'Catholic scouting' by Fr Morgan Crowe, diocesan chaplain.

Fr Morgan Crowe, curate of University Church, who had succeeded Fr
Gallagher as diocesan chaplain in 1952, was, it seems, largely responsible for
setting up the new 'cadet' troop. This and other initiatives which he took
were resented by the National Executive Board, whose members expressed
concern to Archbishop McQuaid at 'a grave strain in relations' between the
Dublin scouts and the National Board. As a result, Fr Crowe was replaced as
diocesan chaplain by Alfred (Alfie) G. Tonge in 1956.

4TH KERRY/1ST LISTOWEL

During World War II and thereafter troops throughout the country were no
less active than those in the archdiocese of Dublin. They instilled self-discipline and self-reliance and provided training in outdoor and other skills. The
extent to which troops enriched the lives of boys both with regard to recre-
ation and to useful activity can be gathered from a pen-picture of any one
of more than a hundred troops The success of troops largely depended on
the imagination, talent and commitment of their leaders. Some were quite
colourful. Few were more so than Michael Kennelly, of the 4th Kerry and
later 1st Listowel troop.

Kennelly served behind the counter in the 'Cloth Hall', a family drap-
ery business. A founder member of the Listowel Drama Group, he co-
authored a number of plays. The 4th Kerry was established in 1931 but
within a few years was wound up when its leaders resigned. Kennelly reorganised it, registered it in 1943 and led it until he retired from scouting in
1953. The troop never had more than thirty members. At the weekly meeting there was drilling and preparation for tests for merit badges: for cycling,
first-aid, horse-riding, interpreting and woodwork. An army instructor
occasionally took members for gymnastics and exercises with Indian clubs.
For some years members were instructed in boxing and took part in a competition with members of other troops at Ballybunion, Killarney and
Tralee. Sunday hikes were organised to scenic spots on the River Feale.

Kennelly was adventurous when it came to planning the troop's annual
camp. At a time when others did not venture much beyond county boundaries he took his troop further afield year after year. In 1944 he took his
scouts for a week's stay in the An Óige hostel in Mountjoy Square. There

were visits to the roof of *Irish Independent* house, the top of Nelson's Pillar, the Botanic Gardens, the Zoo and a football match in Croke Park. In the hostel the troop had a sing-song with seven hikers from the Shankill in Belfast.

In 1945 the annual camp was held partly in Dublin and partly in the An Óige hostel in Enniskerry. This enabled the members to realise that their county did not have a monopoly of Ireland's scenic beauty. In 1946 the annual camp was at Gweedore in County Donegal. The journey to camp involved a flight from Rineanna (later Shannon Airport) to Collinstown (later Dublin Airport) and a journey on a narrow-gauge railway from Letterkenny to Burtonport. In 1947 Kennelly took his troop to camp at Knaresborough, near Harrogate in Yorkshire. The camp was shared with troops from Leeds and Skipton. The English scout leaders had seen active service in the British army and the camp was run along military lines.

In the autumn of 1947 Kennelly was informed that it was not the policy of the CBSI to organise annual camps outside the country. This prompted him almost a year later to affiliate the troop with the B-P scouts and the 4th Kerry became the 1st Listowel Boy Scouts. Thus in 1948 the summer camp was at Gilwell Park, London, training centre of the B-P scouts. There members benefited from rigorous training in basic scouting and had an opportunity to visit the major sights of London and other places such as the nearby Epping Forest.

For summer camp in 1949 the Listowel scouts spent some days in Paris before travelling on to Lourdes. In Paris they were accommodated by Abbé Pierre Conan. He and a troop of boy scouts from his parish of St Severin, near the Sorbonne, had been guests of the Listowel scouts in 1946 and 1948. In 1950 the Listowel troop travelled to Rome for the Holy Year celebrations. After stopovers at Aix-les-Bains and Zurich, they arrived at a huge camp site near the church of St Paul Outside the Walls in Rome. This had been prepared by the Italian Federation of Boy Scouts for scouts arriving from all over the world. Kennelly, in a typical imaginative gesture, at a general audience handed Pius XII a roll of Irish tweed for poor children in Rome.

In 1951 the troop travelled to the 7th World Scout Jamboree at Bad Ischl, near Salzburg. The Listowel scouts and some from Tuam, who travelled with them, were accommodated in the visitors' section of the camp. The jamboree was dominated by American scouts and the US 8th Army seemed to be everywhere helping their compatriots. The journey through Austria, then occupied by the US, USSR, UK and France, and the sight of trains filled with flag-waving communist youth on their way to a huge rally left one in no doubt about the tenuous nature of the post-World-War-II peace in Europe.

Throughout his years as scoutmaster, apart from showing outstanding imagination in choosing destinations for the annual camp, Kennelly was most adept at organising concerts and other functions to subsidise the troop's trips abroad.

LISTOWEL JAMBORETTE, 1948

The most spectacular achievement of Kennelly and his troop was the jamborette in Listowel from 28 July to 10 August 1948. With his life-long friend, Fr Leo Walsh, chaplain and leader of St Anne's troop in Leeds, he planned it when they were together in camp at Knaresborough in 1947.

Scout troops came from Bandon (9th Cork), Ballyhaunis (4th Mayo), Dublin (1st, 4th 19th, 45th, 52nd and 61st Dublin), Dungarvan-Abbeyside (4th Waterford), Galway (1st Galway), Limerick (12th Limerick), Roscommon (4th Roscommon), Thurles (1st Tipperary), and Tuam (2nd Galway). There was a large contingent from Leeds (St Anne's) as well as troops from Skipton (St Stephen's) in Yorkshire, and Paddington (38th West London). France was represented by scout troops from Paris (St Severin) and Rheims (cathedral scout rover crew). The international character of the jamborette was further emphasised by scouts from Austria, Belgium, Czechoslovakia and Italy. Five scout chaplains were with the scouts in camp and provided them with Mass each morning. A camping site for the 500 or more visitors was provided in fields on the bank of the Feale, near the 'big bridge' into the town.

Wartime rationing of food and fuel was still in place. Special permits had to be secured from the department of industry and commerce to ensure that the visitors would not be short of these items. CIE was particularly helpful and provided special train and bus services. The bulk of those attending the jamborette arrived on a special train to Listowel station and marched through the town to the campsite. They were led by four bands. One was the bugle and drum band of the Leeds troop, in which, with a leopard skin over his shoulders, Peter O'Toole, who later becamse a celebrated actor, played the big drum.

With the help of the visiting scout leaders, not least Séamus Durkan, P.J. Grealish, Pierre Langlet and Jim Lydon, the jamborette was organised to provide basic training in scouting. In addition, inter-patrol and inter-troop competitions were held in various sporting activities. There was an international sports day with competitions open to all participants in the jamborette. The valuable trophy for the outstanding sportsman was donated by Claude Jarman, star of the popular Hollywood film, *The Yearling*. A member of the 48th Culver City, California, he sent with the trophy a greeting to his fellow-scouts at the jamborette. Most of the scouts spent a day enjoying a visit to the lakes of Killarney and were given a civic reception in the town of Killarney.

The townspeople enthusiastically supported the jamborette. Various functions, including a football match, were held to raise funds for it. Several open days were arranged at the campsite at which entertainment was provided for the local people. Before the close of the jamborette, a campfire concert was organised, with contributions from the various groups. It was held on part of the dry riverbed near the 'big bridge' from which hundreds of locals were able to enjoy it. The concert was recorded and subsequently broadcast by Radio Éireann.

Initially the national executive board of the CBSI adopted a cautious attitude towards the proposed jamborette. When it opened the executive sent Michael Lawlor, a member of its staff who for over twenty-five years ran the supplies section at 71 St Stephen's Green, to inspect the site. He spent the first weekend in camp and reported positively back to Dublin, whereupon the Chief Scout sent the following greeting to those assembled at the jamborette:

> I wish all a pleasant time in friendship, in full conference and in all scouting endeavour.
>
> With our Irish scouts I would join in welcoming most cordially those troops and officers who honour us by their visit. I trust that they find their time in Ireland of such pleasure and benefit that we may confidently look forward to their return to us in future years.
>
> To the organisers of the jamborette I would extend my personal congratulations on their courage, enterprise and energy. I do hope their efforts shall be recompensed by what I know they have in view – a big advance in Catholic scouting at its best.

The caution exhibited by the national executive board was understandable. At that time the 4th Kerry was only at best a 'maverick' troop. This was the term then in use at headquarters for a non-registered troop. In the event, the pragmatic attitude adopted by the CBSI authorities to the jamborette was typical throughout the association, particularly at troop level. Scout leaders had little interest in the constitution, rules, bureaucracy or 'internal politics' of the organisation. They were simply intent on running their troops in a manner which was most beneficial and enjoyable for their members.

JUBILEE COLLECTION

By 1950 members of the national executive board realised the urgent need for an adequate national training programme. They were also aware that considerable funding would be required to finance it. Thus they decided to organise a nationwide collection in connection with the silver jubilee celebrations of the association.

Paddy Hughes was among those urging that a proper training programme be set up. A senior and much cherished employee of the publishers Browne and Nolan Ltd he began scouting with the 1st Dublin (Fairview). Subsequently he was scoutmaster of the 26th Dublin (Iona Road), which won the Melvin trophy on a number of occasions. He was one of the organisers of the inaugural Dublin diocesan camp at Santry in 1937. Always a pioneer and innovator, he produced a lengthy cine film, *Campa*, of his troop's annual camps during the war years. Popular with his peers, he was most literate, for many years reviewing books for the *Evening Herald*. He was a member of the national executive board, a diocesan commissioner and served as national secretary from 1949 to 1961. With the Chief Scout he had the responsibility of coordinating the collection.

Throughout 1950 the Chief Scout personally canvassed the support of the twenty-six members of the Irish hierarchy. When the Chief Scout and Hughes met Archbishop McQuaid they found him less than enthusiastic about the collection. At that time the archbishop was just about to add a large extension to Holy Cross College, Clonliffe, the diocesan seminary, and was collecting funds to this end. He appealed successfully to his visitors to postpone the CBSI collection for two years and promised his full support thereafter. He was true to his word. Subsequently he introduced and led discussions on the CBSI and, indeed, on all aspects of youth ministry at meetings of the hierarchy. Hughes established a close rapport with the archbishop and was assisted by him in preparing the launch of the fundraising campaign and the accompanying brochure.

The official launch of the national collection was held in the Mansion House on Sunday, 29 November 1953, before a large representative attendance. The following was the agenda:

1. Rt. hon. the lord mayor of Dublin takes chair and speaks.
2. (a) His excellency the president of Ireland moves resolution that:

33. 10th Dublin, St Teresa's troop, Clarendon Street, parading to the Pro-Cathedral in 1940 (Photo. John Graham)

34. Assisting at Knock Shrine, *c.* 1946. *Left to right*: Michael Kennelly, scoutmaster, 4th Kerry, and Séamus Durkan, scoutmaster, 4th Mayo, and later national commissioner

35. Chief Scout presenting the Melvin trophy to 4th Waterford, Abbeyside, in 1958. *Front row, left to right*: Chief Scout, T.C. Egan, assistant commissioner, C.J. Murphy, national commissioner, Peadar Cassidy, vice-president, Fr Dan Gallagher, national chaplain, Walter McGrath, Cork diocesan commissioner, Liam Langan, scoutmaster, 4th Waterford

36. Preliminary training course (PTC) At Ennismore, Cork, in 1959. *Front row, left to right*: J. O'Leary, Con Twomey, Fr Aengus, OFM Cap, J. McGrath, P.T. Hughes, director of training, Fr Enda Gorman, P.J. Killackey, F. Nott

37. Annual meeting of the International Catholic Scout Conference at Gormanston College in 1961. *Front row, left to right*: Fr Frank Callery, *5th*: Philippe Tossijn of the Belgian Vlaams Verbond der Katholique Scouts, the main architect of the Federation of Irish Scout Associations (FISA)

38. Group at training course in Larch Hill in 1962. *Front row, left to right*: John O'Loughlin Kennedy, Fr Billy Fitzgerald, Con Twomey, Fr Paddy O'Reilly, T.P. Hughes, director of training, Stephen Spain, Fr Frank Callery, Fr Colm Matthews, unidentified, P.J. Killackey. *Second row, last on the right*: Fr Aengus, OFM Cap

39. Group at training course in Larch Hill in September 1965, presided over by John Thurman, Camp Chief, Gilwell Park, at which the Wood Badge and Gilwell scarf were presented to all former wearers of the grey neckerchief of the 1st Larch Hill unit. *Front row, left to right*: Séamus Durkan, Con Twomey, unidentified, P.J. Killackey, John Thurman, Fr Frank Callery, unidentified, Dan Tracey. *Second row: 2nd from the right*: Fr Cathal Price

40. First Diocesan Commissioners Conference at the Royal Hotel, Bray, in 1966. *Front row, left to right*: Conal Hooper, P.J. Killackey, Dominic Coleman, national commissioner, Donal McGahon, director of organisation, James Nolan, national secretary. *Second row, left to right*: Michael Redmond, Fred G. Moiselle, Joe Lawlor, unidentified, John O'Brien, Damonn Ó Ceallaigh, Walter McGrath. *Third row, left to right*: unidentified, Ciril Ó Fearghail, Pádraig Ó Broin, Seán O'Connor. *Back row, left to right*: Teeve Carroll, David Maher, Donal O'Sullivan, Hugh McGrath and Frank O'Shea

41. Chief Scout presents the insignia of the Order of the Silver Wolfhound to Jim Hally, director of 'Lios Mór '67'. *Left to right*: Bishop Michael Russell of Waterford and Lismore, Jim Hally and C.J. Murphy

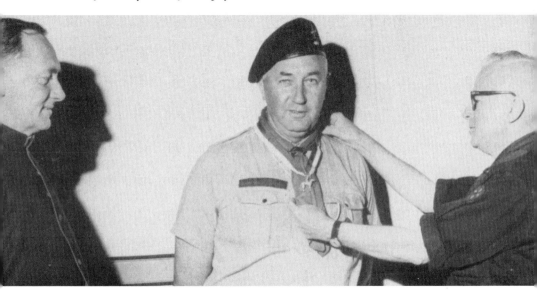

42. Dublin diocesan scout seminar on 'Discipline and self-discipline' at Ely House, April 1968. *Left to right*: Col Patrick Hogan, national executive board, later Chief Scout, Fred Moiselle, Dublin diocesan commissioner, Archbishop John C. McQuaid, Dr M. Carney, UCD, Mgr Cecil Barrett, VG, Walter McGrath, Cork diocesan commissioner

43. President de Valera opens the new Larch Hill House in 1972. *Left to right*: Stephen Spain, Deputy Chief Scout, President de Valera, Paudge Ó Broin, director of Larch Hill

44. 'Jamborora '77' was held at Mount Melleray, County Waterford to honour CBSI's 50th anniversary. Here Archbishop Gaetano Alibrandi, the apostolic nuncio, in centre of picture, visits one of the Italian campsites

45. Sir Patrick Mayhew, Northern Ireland secretary, and Lady Mayhew on the occasion of their visit to 'Ballyfin '93'. *Left to right*: Garth Morrison, Chief Scout, SAUK, Joe Lawlor, Chief Scout, CBSI, Sir Patrick Mayhew, Kiernan Kildea, Camp Chief, Ken Ramsey, Chief Scout, SAI, Robert Sloan, adc to Camp Chief

46. Interim national management committee outside national office, Larch Hill, June 2003. *Front row, left to right*: Peter Dixon, Chief Scout, Scouting Ireland (CSI), Fr Peter Kehoe, O. Carm, national chaplain, Niall Walsh, national treasurer, Martin Burbridge, Chief Scout, Scouting Ireland, Eugene McHugh, chief commissioner, youth programme, Mark O'Callaghan, national secretary, Brendan McNicholas, chief commissioner, adult resources, Donald Harvey, Chief Scout, Scouting Ireland (SAI). *Back row, left to right*: Tony Sweeney, Michael John Shinnock, Jason Horan, Orla McCarthy, international commissioner, Kiernan Gildea, John McCormack, Pat Murphy, Andrew Kelly, Rob Gill, Tony Smith, Derek Watson, Mary Nugent. *Missing from picture*: Christy McCann

47. Scout leaders at Windsor, England, on the occasion of the Queen's Scout Parade on St George's Day, 25 April 2004. *Left to right*: Peter Dixon, Chief Scout, CSI, Donald Harvey, Chief Scout, SAI, George Purdy, Chief Scout, UK Scouts, Martin Burbridge, Chief Scout, SI

The Catholic Boy Scouts of Ireland organisation is worthy of the support of the public.

(b) His eminence the cardinal, primate of All-Ireland seconds motion.

(c) Motion supported by Oscar Traynor, Esq., TD, minister for defence.

(d) Motion supported by Professor C. J. O'Reilly, MA., supreme knight of the Order of the Knights of St Columbanus.
Vote put to meeting from chair.

3. (a) J.A. Costello, Esq., SC., TD., moves that:
A subscription list be now opened to provide a fund to promote the interests and objects of Catholic Scouting in Ireland.

(b) Mr W. Norton, TD, seconds the motion.

(c) Motion supported by::
(i) Senator Baxter, Esq., TD.
Vote put to meeting by chair.

4. (a) His grace the Archbishop of Dublin, primate of Ireland, proposes vote
of thanks to:

The chair and our guest speakers.

(b) His lordship the bishop of Limerick seconds vote of thanks.

(c) Vote supported by Dr J.P. Brennan, master general of the Guild of SS
Luke, Cosmas and Damian.

5. The Chief Scout speaks for the Catholic Boy Scouts of Ireland.

The platform party included the president, the cardinal, the archbishops of Dublin and of Tuam and nine other members of the hierarchy. Apart from the Taoiseach, Eamon de Valera, the leaders of all the political parties were present, as were nine lord mayors from around the country, the commissioner of the Garda Síochána, the chief of staff of the army, the president of UCD and others who were prominent in voluntary social service organisations. Representing the CBSI were Fr Ernest Farrell, PP, national chaplain; Fr Morgan Crowe CC, Dublin diocesan chaplain; Professor Joseph B. Whelehan, Chief Scout; Patrick T. Hughes, Dublin diocesan commissioner and national secretary; and Christopher J. Murphy, national commissioner. The brochure prepared to promote the national collection was just as impressive in its own way as the official launch of the campaign.

Many generous donations were made to the collection, not least by

Archbishop McQuaid and the Knights of St Columbanus, both individually and as a body. However, in view of the expectations which had been raised, the return from the collection was disappointing. Owing to delays and misunderstandings, a proposed fundraising campaign in the US was not even started. Another reason for the appeal's lack of success was the decision to direct it at vocational groups rather than to take up church collections. This was an approach generally favoured by the Knights of St Columbanus. But more importantly, at grassroots level the taking-up of a collection was alien to the culture of scouting. This went right back to the philosophy of Baden-Powell, for whom self-reliance and self-sufficiency were integral parts of scouting. Whenever troops wished to subsidise members when going on their annual camp they invariably earned the money for this by presenting concerts, exhibitions, plays or by providing a service of one kind or another during 'bob-a-job' week. This was what the Chief Scout had in mind when in a letter to Bishop James Fergus of Achonry dated 22 September 1953, he wrote 'at no time in the past twenty-six years has any financial aid come to the Catholic Boy Scouts of Ireland from any sources extern to the organisation'. The antipathy of scouts to collections was reflected in Fr Alfie Tonge's report on the Dublin scouts for 1956. He noted that 'For the last weekend in December the national executive board organised a flag-day collection in the Dublin diocese for their funds. Most of our troops cooperated in this effort, while not altogether agreeing that it was a suitable method of raising funds for scouting purposes'.

REVISED CONSTITUTION 1957

By the mid-1950s, because of legal requirements, changes had to be made to the *Constitution and Rules of the CBSI*. By that time also there was a general consensus among members of the national council that the original constitution should be revised. Most dissatisfaction with it centred on the lack of recognition it gave to the role of the scoutmaster. The local supervising committee, college or school and the chaplain, were, in effect, stated to be in charge of a troop. The scoutmaster was only their appointee, with no role in the control, direction or policy of the troop. This anomaly was only partially rectified. Scoutmasters or principal leaders of units had to wait until 1964 for a further amendment in the constitution, whereby they were admitted to membership of the national council. Moreover, in the revised constitution of 1957 the chaplain was given overall responsibility for the troop. There were other revisions at that time, not least amendments with regard to trustees.

The Chief Scout and national secretary consulted Archbishop McQuaid on the proposed amendments, some of which he further emended. Subsequently they submitted these to him for his approval. This he did after he had their legal accuracy checked. In 1957 the revised *Constitution and Rules of the CBSI* was introduced and immediately became known as the 'Grey Book' because of the colour of its covers. By most scouters it was not regarded as being much of an improvement on its predecessor, the 'Yellow Book', and frequently was honoured more in the breach than in the observance.

NATIONAL TRAINING COURSE

The first national training course was held at Larch Hill on 8–13 September 1956. Twenty-six scout leaders took part and these were drawn from the following districts: Limerick (7), Cork (6), Belfast (5), Dublin (3), Sligo (2), Waterford (2) and Mayo (1). Frs G. Hannon, CSSp, and M. Manning, CC, attended for most of the course but were not counted as full members. The course was conducted by Fr Patrick W. Corrigan,. national Catholic scout chaplain for England and Wales, assisted by his brother, Fr M. A. Corrigan, Birmingham diocesan scout chaplain; W. L. Chesworth, vice-chairman, Birmingham Catholic scout guild and county commissioner; H. Evans, secretary, Birmingham scout guild; H. Davenport, group scoutmaster; and R. Austin, Oxford city commissioner and treasurer of the Catholic scout advisory council. The objective of the course was set out as follows:

> To train scout leaders in the practical application of scouting practices through work in camp and by informal talks on the principles of Catholic scouting. To demonstrate methods by which religion may be integrated in troop meeting places and in camp. To show how a scout leader may further develop boys' Catholic outlook and link them personally with Our Lord, Our Lady and the saints. To emphasise that scouting is not an end in itself but that it is supplementary to the training received at home, in the church and at school.

In his report on the course Hughes commended the enthusiasm of the participants, 48 per cent of whom passed it. But he continued that this success rate was not an indication of scouting standards throughout the country and added: 'A great deal of encouragement will be required before some of the older scoutmasters fully realise their inadequacies and accept the fact that they need such training'. He indicated that in order to retain the interest of those who passed the course an elite troop with a distinctive grey tweed neckerchief and known as the 1st Larch Hill would be formed. Membership would be confined to those who had passed all the training requirements and undertook the following additional obligations:

(1) Maintain the high ideals of Catholic scouting according to the constitution of CBSI.

(2) Maintain the highest possible standards of practical scouting in their troops.

(3) Under the guidance of the Executive Board be responsible for the development and maintenance of the training ground at Larch Hill.

(4) If the above three conditions are not fulfilled, the Executive Board has the power to ask for the neckerchief and membership card of the troop to be returned.

In addition Hughes set out the following programme for the following year:

(1) *Duty to God training course:* A training course to demonstrate the methods suggested for integrating religion with scouting has been arranged by Father Corrigan for 9-11 November next in Liverpool. An invitation has been extended to four Irish participants and I suggest we send two chaplains and two leaders (from the successful twelve).

(2) *Preliminary training course:* An initial week-end course to be held indoors in Larch Hill before the end of January next. This is to be conducted by Father P.W. Corrigan with a staff drawn from the twelve members of the 1st Larch Hill Troop. Immediately after this short course, an intensive grinding of the Irish staff members be given on methods of presentation of Catholic scouting to adult leaders.

(3) *Preliminary training courses:* Three further week-end courses to be held in Limerick, Cork and Belfast and conducted entirely by the Larch Hill troop.

(4) From these four week-end courses, twenty-eight trainees to be selected to form the participation team for an eight-days course in Larch Hill during August next.

(5) *Patrol leaders course:* An outdoor week-end course for patrol leaders of sixteen years and upwards to be held at Whit. It is hoped that this would form the basis of extending principles of the course through the boys themselves. This course to be again run by members of the 1st Larch Hill troop.

(6) *International Catholic scout camp:* The members of the 1st Larch Hill troop to act as the leaders of our contingent and be responsible for the design and erection of the Irish campsite and altar.

(7) *Development of Larch Hill training ground:* Along with the above activities, work must proceed on the development of the training site and
the preparation of the house for the August training course. Plans are
being drawn for the permanent dining shelters, latrines and fireplaces.
These, as I have already indicated, will be comparatively simple structures but will, nevertheless, cost about £50 for the four patrol sites.
Providing we can get enough voluntary labour for the work in Larch
Hill House, our expenditure should not there exceed £100. A list of the
essential work has now been made and we have ensured that any
labour offered will be availed of either at weekends or during winter
evenings.

Hughes emphasised that the object of the training was to build a team
capable of keeping in touch with up-to-date trends in the presentation of
Catholic scouting. He added that to achieve this they would be dependent
on outside help for some time to come. Next he illustrated how the CBSI's
lack of access to international scouting was a serious disadvantage with
regard to training:

Associations recognised by the International Bureau may avail of the services of an international training team in setting up and maintaining training courses for their leaders. This international training team is composed
of professional scouters who are dependent for their livelihood on their
skill in keeping up-to-date on methods of presentation. It is difficult, if
not impossible, for the amateur depending on limited spare time to keep
contact with methods adapted to changing circumstances. When CBSI
was founded in 1926, there were few competing attractions for teen-age
boys and less temptation to test their Faith. CBSI has not kept pace with
changing times but now realises the importance of meeting the real danger of losing touch with the present generation of boyhood.

In the meantime he recommended that those who had been trained at the
Larch Hill courses should be given the opportunity of gaining further expe-
rience at the French Catholic scout training camp or at the German or
Dutch centres. This was feasible, he continued, as they had good relations
with Catholic scout associations throughout Europe and with the Catholic
division of the Boy Scouts of America. In the event a number, including Fr
Paddy Dowling, Fr Enda Gorman, Fr Paddy O'Reilly and John O'Loughlin
Kennedy, did attend the French Catholic scout training camp (*Camp de
Campisme, Scouts de France*) at Jambville, near Paris. Others, including Patrick

J. Killackey, went to the International Training Centre at Gilwell Park, near London.

Hughes faced considerable opposition to his efforts to have the training programme he proposed implemented. This came mainly from within the Dublin diocesan training committee. From 1946 onwards this committee each spring held outdoor training in practical scouting and leadership at Larch Hill and this was supplemented by a series of appropriate lectures and film-shows during the winter. One result of the opposition of members of this committee, who were also members of the Dublin Diocesan Council, was the poor attendance of Dublin scout leaders at the first national training course. It was also significant that the two Dublin scout leaders who took the course successfully were subsequently not elected on to the Dublin diocesan training team. In a letter to the archbishop, dated 17 July 1957, Hughes complained: 'Last year a wave of antipathy swept over Dublin against the "importation of Englishmen" to teach our scoutmasters the mechanics of their scouting and this has not been wholly eradicated.'

Although this was not mentioned by Hughes, objections to the personnel of the national training course were not the only source of opposition to it. The fact that it was seen as superseding the annual Dublin diocesan training course was resented, as was the emphasis on the B-P 'patrol system'. The course was conducted in accordance with the *Ki-Ro handbook*. This had been published by the Catholic Scout Association of England and Wales, and suggested methods whereby religious training would be incorporated into scouting practice. Some scout leaders were sceptical as to its suitability in training courses for Irish scouts. They were not alone in this. In his report for 1957, the Dublin diocesan chaplain, Fr Alfie Tonge, wrote: 'The value in practice of Ki-Ro seems more apparent than real, when applied to scouts who practically all are well versed in their religion through the system of catechetics in their school – primary and technical – in this diocese'. The archbishop had already reached that conclusion and, at his suggestion, a committee of scout chaplains had been charged with examining 'the Ki-Ro system of catechetics' and producing an alternative more suitable for the diocese of Dublin. However, only preliminary steps ere taken to produce this alternative.

Notwithstanding the opposition, Hughes succeeded in implementing the programme on national training. He was strongly supported by Archbishop McQuaid, who, at his invitation, paid brief visits to Larch Hill to meet those taking part in the courses. After one such visit the archbishop was 'shocked' at the poor condition of Larch Hill House and sent

Hughes a large donation to improve its facilities. He also ensured that the Catholic Social Service Conference of the archdiocese generously subsidised the training courses at Larch Hill. Hughes was particularly successful in organising the preliminary training courses (PTCs), usually of weekend duration, in the provinces. They were invariably held in the grounds of the houses of religious. One such course, at the Benedictine Glenstal Abbey, Murroe, near Limerick, in January 1962, was memorable in that for the first time the CBSI appeared on national television. In the meantime the main national training course had become popular, as scout leaders were eager for membership of the 1st Larch Hill and the privilege to wear its much coveted grey tweed neckerchief. The annual national training course continued and in September 1965 was accredited with Gilwell recognition after a special inaugural course led by R. F. (John) Thurman, one of the Gilwell Park Training Centre's most famous camp chiefs.

Thurman was a professional scouter and an expert in many facets of scouting, including 'ropes and spars'. He stressed the importance of the 'patrol system of scouting'. This meant that each patrol took responsibility for all their activities: camping, cooking, planning and organising events etc. This was regarded as the best way to develop qualities of leadership, self-sufficiency and independence. It was the distinctive element inherited from Baden-Powell that made scouting more effective than other youth organisations; highlighting its importance had also been a focus of all the national training courses from 1956 onwards.

CHAPLAINS

The leadership of the CBSI realised that chaplains could play a crucial role in raising standards of discipline and achievement in troops. They were also aware that, while troops throughout the country had chaplains, these, for the most part, did not become involved in the running of troops or in their scouting activities. It was generally agreed this situation could be improved by encouraging young priests who had been scouts and/or who had a propensity for the outdoor life and scouting to be chaplains. To this end, from 1957 onwards the Dublin diocesan chaplain and the 1st Larch Hill or national training team spent a 'scout day' at Clonliffe College. They presented the elements of scouting to the senior seminarians and suggested to them that chaplaincy to a scout troop was an admirable form of youth ministry. From the following year the national training team also visited St Patrick's College, Maynooth, and St Peter's College, Wexford, for this purpose. This proved to be worthwhile. Beginning in 1957 newly ordained priests showed a much greater appreciation than previously of scouting. Also a number of young priests took up posts of responsibility in the CBSI, apart from acting as troop or scout chaplains.

No one was more eager that chaplains should be suitable and properly prepared than Archbishop McQuaid. He enthusiastically supported the initiative of presenting scouting in the seminaries. He also cooperated with Hughes in organising a midweek national chaplains' conference. The first of its kind, it was held in the Grand Hotel, Greystones, County Wicklow, in October 1959. Thirty-nine chaplains attended, thirteen from Dublin archdiocese, seventeen from other dioceses and nine from various religious congregations or orders. Among the lecturers were: Fr Michael Clarke, a former professor in Holy Cross College, Clonliffe; Fr Patrick W. Corrigan, national Catholic scout chaplain for England and Wales; Fr John C. Kelly, SJ; Rev Professor Gerard Montagu, St Patrick's College, Maynooth; and Rev Professor E. F. O'Doherty, UCD. The conference was opened by the archbishop and ended with Solemn Benediction imparted by the papal nuncio, Dr Antonio Riberi. The papal nuncio had expressed to Hughes a wish to visit the conference, when he invited him to the nunciature a week earlier. He told Hughes of his 'long interest in the Catholic scout movement' and that 'the Italian Catholic body had been re-established in his Roman villa at the end of the war'.

In his keynote address the archbishop sounded a discordant note. It seems he was irked by a fanfare of publicity about the conference which had appeared in the press, especially the provincial papers. Perhaps he also disliked the prospect of being overshadowed by the papal nuncio. He indicated that he did not wish to be reported. It soon became clear why. He compared the CBSI unfavourably with the B-P scouts and criticised the CBSI programme for its lack of content, a lack of emphasis on discipline and a lack of purpose, and he was scathing about the appearance of some members of the CBSI. 'You have failed', he continued, 'to develop an officer class because the secondary schools have never accepted you'. He suggested that the CBSI had 'fallen between two stools – a military organisation and a club for hobbies'. His words were not well received, especially by the priests from other dioceses. There was far less enthusiasm for the second national conference of chaplains which was also held at Greystones, in November 1960. And it is significant that no further such conferences were organised until 1967.

PATRICIAN YEAR, 1961

The Irish hierarchy nominated 1961 as a Patrician Year. Celebrations were held throughout the country to mark the fiteen-hundredth anniversary of the death of St Patrick and to honour his mission to Ireland. Members of the CBSI provided stewarding and guards of honour at liturgical celebrations and other ceremonies. However their involvement in the celebrations in Dublin was minimal.

The main celebration in Dublin was a congress held in June in the National Boxing Stadium. Eminent lay Catholics from abroad lectured at the congress. Numerous distinguished ecclesiastics, including Cardinal Agaginian, who acted as papal legate, attended it. Throughout the congress period they presided at Masses and other liturgical functions in various parishes. Fr G. Thomas Fehily was the congress director. At the beginning of 1961 he held discussions with the CBSI leadership with regard to the provision of stewarding and guards of honour at the congress events and venues. Because of the number of these, the CBSI were not able to guarantee a scout presence at many of them, whereupon Fr Fehily raised what he termed a congress volunteer corps (CVC). This was a group of between 150 and 200 fifth-year students from the Catholic secondary schools. In time for the Congress they were provided with a uniform in the papal colours and training in drill and crowd control. After the congress they were known as the Archbishop's Volunteer Corps (AVC) and later as the Colleges Volunteer Corps (CVC). From 1972 onwards girls were admitted to the ranks. For over forty years the CVC have attended major ecclesiastical celebrations in Dublin. In addition, members have accompanied the annual diocesan pilgrimage to Lourdes and some have helped in the running of youth clubs and the provision of help to the elderly.

OTHER PUBLICATIONS

In October 1959 the first issue of the *Scout Leader* appeared. It was essentially a vehicle for communicating information from headquarters to scout leaders throughout the country. In 1962 *Come scouting* was published. Edited by Donal McGahon and Fr John MacMahon, it set out the requirements for qualifying as a rawly scout, a second class scout and a first class scout.

Most importantly of all, *The Scouting Trail: the Official Scout Handbook*, also edited by Donal McGahon and Fr John MacMahon, appeared in 1965. Its official launch on 23 February was overshadowed by the state funeral of Sir Roger Casement. While the state funeral closed a chapter in the country's history, the new handbook inaugurated a new phase in the history of the CBSI.

Much effort had been put into the production of the new handbook. In 1960 the National Executive Board, realising that the original badge scheme was in urgent need of revision, set up a subcommittee, known as the badges, rewards and requirements committee (BAR Committee), to carry out the work. Fr John MacMahon was appointed secretary to the committee, the aim of which was to produce a programme calculated to bring out qualities of leadership in boys and to interest them at the same time. Members of the committee studied the programmes of Catholic scout organisations in Belgium, England and Wales, France, Germany, Holland, Italy, Switzerland and the US. They consulted widely among chaplains and scout leaders throughout the CBSI. In less than two years the final draft was passed by the national executive board and the national council. In January 1962 Archbishop McQuaid, in effect on behalf of the hierarchy, expressed himself satisfied with its religious content. On Sunday, 11 March 1962, it was submitted to a meeting of the country's scout leaders in the Shelbourne Hotel, Dublin. In his address to over 200 uniformed scoutmasters, Peadar Cassidy, Deputy Chief Scout, set the tone of the meeting by saying: 'We exist for the boy and for his welfare. He is the be-all and the end-all of our endeavours'. Fr John MacMahon introduced the new tests. Other changes which had been proposed were also explained. Some regrets were expressed at the disappearance of 'My Land' as the scout anthem, the papal dates from rawly tests and semaphore and 'scout pace' from the second class tests. But there was overwhelming support and acceptance for the new handbook. This was the beginning of a series of changes and revisions in 'programme activities', which were incorporated into the 2nd and revised edition of 1979 and the 3rd and revised edition of 2003, *The Scouting Trail: a Field Handbook for Scouts*. In the meantime another publication, *CBSI Ceremonies*, edited by Donal MacGahon, had appeared in 1979. It set out guidelines for ceremonies on various occasions and at different venues.

OTHER CHANGES

There were other changes at this time. In 1961 James Nolan succeeded Paddy Hughes as national secretary and in 1962 Christopher J. (Kit) Murphy succeeded Professor Whelehan as Chief Scout. Murphy began his scouting with the headquarters troop. Later he was a member of the national council and national executive board. He also served as national commissioner. In scout circles he was known for his devotion to Lourdes pilgrimages. As a result of his frequent service at the shrine and baths for the sick, he had the privilege of wearing the cherished white neckerchief of the 1st Lourdes troop. He was also a lifelong member of the Knights of St Columbanus.

Also in 1962 also the new national headquarters was opened at 19

Herbert Place. The change from 71 St Stephen's Green marked the departure from CBSI employment of Michael Lawlor. A most popular official, he had presided over a supply centre there from the early years. Subsequently a scout shop was opened in North Frederick Street, later at 14 Fownes Street, and uniform depots were established in Belfast, Cork and Limerick. At this time also women leaders were introduced into the *macaoimh* (cub) section of the association, regularising an initiative of P .J. Killackey and his wife Brigid.

NATIONAL PILGRIMAGES

The centenary of Our Lady's apparition to St Bernadette in Lourdes was celebrated in 1958. It occasioned the most memorable pilgrimage undertaken by the CBSI, its third national pilgrimage to Lourdes. Planned for two years under the supervision of Fr Stephen Greene, chaplain to the 43rd Dublin, the all-scout pilgrim group numbered over one thousand. It was the greatest single 'airlift' carried out by Aer Lingus. Archbishop Joseph Walsh of Tuam led the pilgrimage, Christopher J. (Kit) Murphy, national commissioner, was the Chief Brancardier, and members of the national executive board, including Chief Scout Whelehan and National Chaplain Fr Dan Gallagher, accompanied it. The national executive board organised an equally impressive national scout pilgrimage to the Shrine of Our Lady of Knock in 1960.

CHAPTER FIVE

Towards Unification

CBSI AND INTERNATIONAL CATHOLIC SCOUT CONFERENCE

IN THE EARLY YEARS their non-affiliation to the World Scout Conference, the biennial delegate conference which is the ruling body of the World Organisation of the Scout Movement (WOSM), was not of much concern to the CBSI. They applied for affiliation on two occasions but were informed that this was not possible, as their organisation extended over two national jurisdictions, that of the Irish Free State and Northern Ireland. On the two occasions, first the 12th Earl of Meath and later the 8th Viscount Powerscourt informed the ruling body that the CBSI was disqualified from membership for this reason.

After World War II there was much greater pressure, especially at the grassroots, to establish a link with international scouting. The topic was discussed more and more animatedly at the annual meetings of the national council. In the 1950s Fr Enda Gorman established close links with the *Scouts de France*. Born in Thurles on 9 April 1920, educated at St Patrick's College, Thurles, the Irish College, Paris and St Patrick's College, Maynooth and ordained in 1944, he was a life-long scout enthusiast. He served as a curate in the parishes of Borrisoleigh, Solohead and Bansha. From 1944 until he died on 1 September 1972 he was Cashel diocesan scout chaplain. Fr Gorman was appointed the first international commissioner, and in this capacity he established a link with the International Catholic Scout Conference. This had been set up in 1945 and thereafter its meetings were held in a different country each year.

The issue of the ambiguous international status of the CBSI was highlighted at a meeting of the 11th International Catholic Scout Conference in 1956, which was held in Edinburgh and presided over by Fr W. D. Hamilton, the Scottish national scout chaplain. At the meeting he refused to give the CBSI representatives a vote and stated that, as they were not internationally recognised, they had no right to participate officially in the conference. He suggested that by his action 'the matter of Ireland could [thereby] be brought to a head'. Fr Hamilton went on to allege that the CBSI's 'non-recognition' was due to the 'unreasonable' stand taken by the Archbishop of Dublin who refused on 'several' occasions to discuss any possibility of the CBSI's membership of the World Scout Conference. Paddy Hughes, one of the CBSI's delegates, had little difficulty in dismissing this unfounded allegation. In addition, he set out for the conference and for Dick Lund, an observer from the World Scout Bureau, the central office of WOSM, the circumstances which blocked the CBSI's affiliation to the world body. The conference reversed Fr Hamilton's decision and thereafter there was never any question as to the CBSI's full membership of the International Catholic Scout Conference. Subsequently Hughes provided a detailed account for Fr Hamilton on how the CBSI viewed itself at that time. He also sent a copy of this letter to the delegations to the conference (See Appendix 1).

At this time there was considerable disquiet within the International Catholic Scout Conference about the attitude of the World Scout Bureau to Catholic associations. The bureau had strenuously opposed the formation of Catholic scout organisations in South America. Even the transfer of the Bureau from London to Ottawa was viewed with suspicion. One reason and perhaps the most important reason for the transfer was the devaluation of sterling. Yet while the transfer was welcomed as an indication that the bureau would no longer be under undue 'British imperial influence', several European delegations suspected that the move was dictated by a determination to increase the influence of international freemasonry on scout headquarters. To counter this, the French association proposed the establishment of an International Catholic Scout Council. As this was seen as a potential alternative to the World Bureau, it was rejected by scout associations from countries where Catholics were in a minority, not least the Catholic Scouts of America. In the event, a compromise was arrived at, whereby an International Catholic Scout Committee was set up, in effect to monitor the policy of the World Bureau *vis-à-vis* Catholic associations. From the outset the CBSI was represented on this committee. In 1960 the CBSI received a request to host the annual meeting of the International Catholic Conference, but pleaded lack of readiness to do so. However, in 1961 they organised it very successfully at the Franciscan College in Gormanston, County Meath.

STEPS TOWARDS FEDERATION

Over the years Fr Enda Gorman developed close relationships with several of the delegates to the International Catholic Scout Conference. Among those he met at the this internation forum was Phillipe Tossijn. A Belgian from the Vlaams Verbond der Katholique Scouts, he was a member of the World Scout Committee, the executive of the World Scout Conference, and the executive of the International Catholic Scout Conference. In Belgium there were six scout associations, not least because of language differences. However, they formed a national federation and were in that way affiliated to the World Scout Conference. Tossijn suggested to Fr Gorman that a federation of the B-P scouts (Boy Scouts of Ireland) and the CBSI affiliated to the World Scout Conference would provide the CBSI with the access to international scouting membership it desired.

By the beginning of the 1960s there was general agreement in the CBSI that federation with the Boy Scouts of Ireland (BSI) and thereby affiliation with the World Scout Conference could no longer be delayed. In 1961 the Chief Scout, Professor Joseph B. Whelehan, had to resign owing to ill-health. He was never other than neutral on the issue. Christopher J. (Kit) Murphy, who succeeded him in 1962, was an enthusiastic supporter of federation. By that time the World Scout Bureau was also in favour of a federal arrangement which would facilitate the affiliation of the CBSI. Always eager to have scout associations under their umbrella, if for no other reason than to direct their policies and to have their affiliation fees, they had become aware that the CBSI scouts were more numerous than their B-P counterparts.

For their part the leadership of the BSI responded to a change of mood at grass-roots level. The pontificate of Pope John XXIII had inaugurated an ecumenical climate. The BSI leadership, which represented boys from less than ten per cent of the population, had become conscious that their claim to represent Irish scouting was becoming increasingly untenable. They also realised that this view had become prevalent at the World Scout Bureau. Thus in a letter to Fr Liam Martin, dated 1 March 1959, Paddy Hughes wrote: 'Incidentally, while I was in Belgium last month Phillipe Tossijn, the international commissioner, told me that the Boy Scouts of Ireland representative, E. Montgomery, was nominated for membership of the International Bureau Committee last year. Despite strong support from Britain, Montgomery got only two votes and was not elected.'

NEGOTIATIONS

After the ground had been prepared informally, representatives of the BSI (B-P scouts) and the CBSI were invited to a meeting at B-P House in London on 6 April 1963. Subsequently those who attended were provided with the following memorandum:

> On the initiative of the World Scout Committee, an informal meeting took place in London on 6 April 1963, of members of the Boy Scouts of Ireland, Boy Scouts Association and Catholic Boy Scouts of Ireland, under the chairmanship of M. Phillipe Tossijn, member of the World Committee and of the executive committee of the International Catholic Boy Scout Conference. The director of the World Bureau, Maj. Gen. D.C. Spry, was also present.

As a result of the discussions which took place it was felt desirable to investigate further the possibility of establishing some form of federation of BSI and CBSI so as to make it possible for CBSI to participate fully in the world brotherhood of scouting. The suggestion was for a type of 'nominal' federation which, while leaving each party completely free of interference from the other, would provide a single, small 'federation committee' to which the official recognition of the World Scout Bureau could be extended. Thus recognition would be extended to each member-association of the proposed federation without infringing on its individual autonomy.

> The World Conference Constitution permits the recognition of only one national scout organisation in each country and it would therefore be necessary for recognition to be transferred from BSI to the proposed federation. There appears to be no obstacle to such transfer as far as the World Committee are concerned.

The general feeling was that the following steps should be taken:
(1) BSI and CBSI members should consult their respective executive committees and appoint representatives to discuss further details concerning the proposed federation. CBSI would also require ecclesiastical approval.
(2) After agreement between the two groups on mutually acceptable principles and the details of the federation, BSI would request the World Committee to transfer its recognition to the proposed federation. This transfer would be approved by the World Committee and the parties so informed.
(3) Immediately following the transfer of recognition, arrangements would be made to establish training facilities. World Bureau services

and information would be made available to both parties through the federation committee.

It was felt that the following provisions should be included in the constitution of the proposed federation:

(1)   A statement of assent by the two constituent associations.

(2)   Suggested title: 'Federation of Irish Scout Associations'.

(3)   Acceptance of the aims and fundamental principles of the boy scout movement as contained in the constitution of the world conference. (These are already more than adequately covered in CBSI rules.)

(4)   That the details of the *modus operandi* be worked out by the representatives of BSI and CBSI.

(5)   That the constitution of the proposed federation might be amended by the mutual consent of the two parties to the federation.

At the conclusion of the meeting the director of the World Bureau expressed his appreciation of the evident desire for cooperation displayed at the meeting.

The following attended:

Boy Scouts Association:	Lt Col R. Gold
	J.F. Colquhoun, OBE
Boy Scouts of Ireland:	E.J. Montgomery
	P.C. Scott
Catholic Boy Scouts of Ireland	C.J. Murphy
	P. Cassidy
	J. Nolan
World Committee and Committee of International Catholic Scout Conference:	P. Tossijn (Belgium)
Director, World Bureau:	Maj Gen D.C. Spry (Canada)

The BSI organised an international conference of scout commissioners at Malahide, County Dublin from 18–23 May 1964. On the day following the conference, representatives of the BSI and CBSI met Maj. Gen. D.C. Spry and Phillipe Tossijn. Fr Alfie Tonge, Dublin diocesan chaplain, also attended the meeting. He did so as an observer and representative of Archbishop McQuaid. The meeting formally endorsed the decisions taken a year earlier. It was also agreed that representatives of both associations would present the proposals for federation to their respective memberships and draft a constitution in accordance with the proposals. (For the memorandum prepared and presented to the national council of the CBSI to secure its approval for the federation, see Appendix 2). Just a month later Archbishop

McQuaid briefed his colleagues in the hierarchy at their June meeting on the proposal to form a federation of the two scout associations. When the draft constitution of the new federation became available he presented it to a meeting of the standing committee of the hierarchy in January 1965 and they approved it. Following separate and joint meetings of the associations in 1963, 1964 and 1965 the draft constitution was finally approved and on 1 March 1965 the Federation of Irish Scout Associations (*Co-Chumann Gasóga na hÉireann*) was established. On behalf of the CBSI, Kit Murphy, the Chief Scout wrote in the *Scout Leader* of March 1965:

> I am happy to welcome the formation of the Federation of Irish Scout Associations. It has been recognised by the Boy Scout World Committee and through our membership we are now linked with scouting around the globe and are more than ever a part of the great world brotherhood of close on nine-and-a-half million members. CBSI can now be repre- sented at world jamborees and other big international scout events. I extend greetings to our fellow members of the Federation, the Boy Scouts of Ireland, whose kindness and cooperation have been such a feature of the discussions leading up to the formation of the Federation.

At the meeting of the CBSI National Council, after the federation had been formed, the contribution of Phillipe Tossijn to its establishment was acknowledged, when the Chief Scout inducted him as a member of the Order of the Silver Wolfhound, the first overseas scout to receive the CBSI's premier honour. The first committee of FISA included: (for CBSI) Christopher J. Murphy, Chief Scout; Fr Daniel P. Gallagher, national chap- lain; Fr Enda Gorman, international commissioner; James Nolan, national secretary; and Desmond J. Fay; for BSI: Edward Montgomery, Jack H. Webb, Percy Scott, W. Ernest Judge and John Connell.

Within ten years such were the growing ties between the Irish scout and guide associations that the Chief Scout of CBSI was appointed vice-presi- dent of the SAI (Scout Association Ireland [former BSI]) and of NISC (Northern Ireland Scout Council), and the Chief Scout of SAI and Chief Commissioner of NISC became vice-presidents of CBSI. In addition the Chief Commissioners of the Irish Girl Guides and Ulster Girl Guides and the National Commissioners of the Catholic Guides of Ireland were appointed vice-presidents of CBSI.

DUBLIN CBSI, 1961–71

From 1930 onwards the national council of the CBSI at its annual meeting pledged the continuing loyalty of the delegates to the Archbishop of Dublin. During his time as archbishop, John Charles McQuaid was a strong supporter of the association and this annual pledge was a formal acknowledgement of this. By the beginning of the 1960s, however, he was becoming increasingly frustrated at the failure of the CBSI to link up with colleges and secondary schools and at what he regarded as a lack of urgency in ensuring the proper training of leaders. When consulted by Fr Dan Gallagher, national scout chaplain, with regard to a suitable successor to the ailing Chief Scout, he wrote in a letter dated 31 October 1961: 'The whole position needs review. I have always believed, since first I established a scout company, that the organisation loses in efficiency, because it is not a federation of diocesan groups, in which each diocesan group is an independent unit'. Just a year later, at his request, Fr Alfie Tonge, Dublin diocesan scout chaplain, submitted a detailed report on 'the scouting situation in the diocese of Dublin'.

In his report Fr Tonge expressed the view that 'to have a really strong and well organised scout association it should be based on and controlled by the diocese'. He considered that it had been a mistake to have formed the CBSI with its national council and national executive board. Among the difficulties which this posed for scouts in the Dublin diocese was 'interference' and 'young priests with little experience given prematurely positions of authority on the national executive board'. Fr Tonge acknowledged that it would not be easy to change the administrative structure of the CBSI and that to set up parallel structures at diocesan level would merely complicate matters. He suggested there should be a 'federating council to link up the scouts of different dioceses in their activities' but cautioned that this should not be 'a controlling body'.

In the absence of a radical change in the association's structures, he suggested that the following would be of benefit to Catholic scouting in Dublin:

(1) The national executive board should deal with troops only through the diocesan chaplains, his committee or commissioners.
(2) The provision of a good senior course for boys from fifteen to eighteen years, at which age scouting most affects character.
(3) The position of the chaplain of the troop to be more clearly defined.
(4) Recruiting and appointing of troop chaplains with an interest in scouting.
(5) Once in two years there should be a 'scout day' in the seminary to create this interest.

(6) There are fifty troops in the diocese of Dublin. The great need is for properly trained leaders. If the diocese were divided into two sections, north and south, and an assistant diocesan chaplain appointed to each section under the diocesan chaplain these three could do a lot for scouting.

This was not the first time that such suggestions had been made. In a letter to the archbishop, dated 24 July 1960, Paddy Hughes, national secretary, strongly urged him to appoint a 'full-time' assistant diocesan scout chaplain but Dr McQuaid was dissuaded from doing so by his advisers.

In a letter dated 26 January 1965 the archbishop told Fr Tonge that years earlier he had reached the diocesan chaplain's conclusions but had not been in a position to implement his desires with regard to the CBSI. But he expressed his intention to do so. He began by appointing Fr John MacMahon and Fr Seán O'Sullivan as assistant diocesan scout chaplains to the troops north and south of the Liffey respectively.

In 1964, when the national executive board discussed the changes in the constitution and rules required by the federation with the Boy Scouts of Ireland, members proposed that the rule whereby the national chaplain was elected annually by the board should be changed and that the national chaplain should be appointed by the hierarchy on the recommendation of the archbishop of Dublin. When informed of the proposal, McQuaid, on behalf of his colleagues, agreed to it and on his recommendation, Fr Alfie Tonge succeeded Fr Gallagher. However, at the first meeting of the national executive board that Fr Tonge attended in this capacity the board proposed that 'the position of national chaplain should be held by a bishop' and directed the Chief Scout to meet Bishop James Fergus, secretary of the hierarchy's standing committee, to discuss the matter. In a letter dated 14 September 1967, Fr Tonge informed Dr McQuaid that this was in no way a sign of opposition to his appointment and was merely an example of the national executive board 'seeking for greater notice'. In the event the matter was quietly dropped.

When Fr Tonge was appointed national chaplain Fr John MacMahon succeeded him as Dublin diocesan chaplain and Fr John O'Connell replaced him as assistant diocesan chaplain. In the period from 1961 to 1971 the three diocesan chaplains did much to energise the association in Dublin. The number of troops rose from fifty to sixty-eight. Many of the new leaders were members of the Catholic lay organisation, the Legion of Mary, who ran or helped to run troops as their weekly commitment to apostolic work.

Large rallies of the combined troops north of the Liffey and south of the river were held. They organised a Dublin diocesan symposium in April 1966 at Ely House which was attended by over 200 scout leaders and chaplains. The purpose of the symposium was to remind scout leaders that in Catholic scouting the religious input was at least as important as the basic elements of scouting. Fr Forde, OMI, spoke on 'Understanding the Boy', Dermot O'Flynn on 'The scouter as a lay apostle', Patrick Walsh on 'Development of Leadership in Oneself and then in Others' and Fr Thomas Finnegan of St Patrick's College, Maynooth, on 'Religion through the Scout Promise and tests'. Fr MacMahon and his colleagues helped to organise a national conference of scout chaplains at Greystones in April 1967. Fr O'Sullivan acted as chaplain to the Irish contingent, in which both CBSI and BSI were represented, to the World Scout Jamboree at Idaho, US, in August 1967. The Dublin diocesan chaplains organised an all-day scout seminar on 'Discipline and Self-discipline' at Ely House in April 1968. This was opened by the archbishop, attended by some 250 scout leaders and chaplains and addressed by Dr Michael Carney, department of psychology, UCD; Lt Col Patrick D. Hogan, national executive board; and Walter McGrath, Cork diocesan commissioner. And from 1966 onwards they organised a diocesan-wide cub dedication day each May and a scout dedication day each October.

The chaplains were in no way complacent with regard to the progress which had been made. On 18 March 1968 Fr MacMahon concluded his annual report for 1967 to the archbishop:

> There is a considerable fall off in membership at the thirteen to fifteen age group. It is also to be noted that the majority of our boys do not advance much in scouting skills; only 431 are of 2nd class standard and a mere seventy-four are of 1st class standard. These two problems need to be tackled with energy during the coming year.

NATIONAL CAMPS: LIOS MÓR 1967; JAMBORORA 1977; VISIT OF JOHN PAUL II 1979

The proposal for a national camp at Lios Mór to mark the fortieth anniversary of the establishment of the CBSI was accepted by the national executive board in June 1965. Its main advocate was James D. Hally, a long-serving member of the board, and he undertook to act as camp chief. Through the generosity of the 11th Duke of Devonshire the camp was held on the banks of the Blackwater outside Lismore, County Waterford, hence its name. The camp was attended by 3,000 scouts from 18 to 29 July 1967. On the Sunday of the camp a special Mass was celebrated on the site by Bishop Michael Russell, a life-long supporter of scouting, and seventeen troop chaplains. Also on that Sunday Jack Lynch, the Taoiseach, Liam Cosgrave, leader of Fine Gael, and Brendan Corish, leader of the Labour Party, visited the camp. Cosgrave regaled his hosts with recollections of the national pilgrimage to Rome in 1934, as did Corish of his years in 1st Wexford. As part of the closing ceremony of Lios Mór 1967, Jim Hally was presented with the Order of the Silver Wolfhound, the CBSI's highest award in recognition of his successful running of the camp, as was Bishop Michael Russell.

Jamborora 1977 was the CBSI's celebration of fifty years of scouting. It was held in the grounds of the Cistercian monastery at Mount Melleray, County Waterford, from 26 July to 4 August. The infrastructure of the site was prepared by the army's 1st Field Company of Collins Barracks, Cork. Over 12,000 scouts, including contingents from Italy, Norway, France and the US, as well as representative groups of girl guides attended. The stated aim of the camp was 'to manifest the scouting ideal through activities which incorporates fun, friendship, challenge, education, team spirit and international awareness and consequently creating an environment of true brotherhood and friendship'. The central theme of the camp was Irish history and its seven sub-camps were named after the seven ancient Irish kingdoms: Aileach, Eamhain Macha, Dal Riada, Caiseal, Cruachan, Tara and Deise. Among the camp's activities were pioneering, water activities, skill-o-rama, handcrafts, campcraft and technology. At the skill-o-rama base one could be tested in hurling and football skills, compass-work, tent-pitching, archery, backwoods cooking, model making, semaphore and other skills. There were novelty items such as helicopter, fireworks, and parachute-jumping displays. Apart from the usual sing-along campfires, the scouts and their parents were entertained by traditional groups, including Horslips, Seisiún and The Chieftains. The closing ceremony was performed by Edouard Duvigneaud of the World Scout Committee.

The experience derived from organising the Jamborora proved to be an admirable preparation for the CBSI's participation in the pastoral visit of Pope John Paul II to Ireland from 29 September to 1 October 1979. The CBSI helped with the preparation for the visit and were prominent at the Papal Masses at the Phoenix Park, Dublin, Drogheda, Knock, Galway and Limerick. At these venues they were involved in providing first-aid, stewarding and guards of honour. They were also employed as assistants at the communications and press centres. Like the hundreds of thousands who attended the papal events, members of the CBSI were delighted with the opportunity to express loyalty to their Faith and the Holy Father. On their behalf Bishop Michael Russell, vice-president of CBSI, presented to John Paul II a handsome silver and gold replica of the historic Cross of Cong as a memento of his visit.

CONSTITUTIONAL MATTERS

From the outset scoutmasters were aware of the need to adapt the programme rules, and constitution of the CBSI to changing social conditions. The need to change became particularly acute in the 1960s. At that time a number of conferences of scoutmasters were held to this purpose. Fr Enda Gorman had a prominent role in organising these conferences. Apart from conferences of scoutmasters he helped to organise conferences of diocesan commissioners, the first of which was held in the Royal Hotel, Bray in 1966.

As a result of the widespread consultation fostered by the conferences of scoutmasters, the national council in 1964 voted to include two amendments in the constitution. The first was to admit to membership of the national council the scoutmaster or principal leader of each unit. The second limited the maximum term of office of the Chief Scout to six years. Other proposals from these conferences urged a fundamental evaluation of the structures required to meet boys' current needs. These persuaded the national council to set up a committee in 1968 to review the constitution of 1957. In its report it accepted the unit rather than the troop as the basic element of the association and the need to co-ordinate 'the adult elements in scouting', in effect the scout committee and scoutmaster, into a team. It also recommended that chaplains have a consultative rather than a controlling role and participation by scoutmasters at all levels. The report was adopted in 1969 and the new *Constitution and Rules* came into effect in the following year. There followed a period of intense organisation in each diocese or region. The national executive board concentrated on preparing an up-to-date programme suitable for adult members. Stephen Spain, national commissioner, emphasised the educational nature of scouting and urged that the progression of the child from section to section be further encouraged. However, the new *Constitution and Rules* was not considered to be sufficiently radical by those urging constitutional reform, and, bowing to their demands, the national council appointed a Constitution Review Commission in 1978.

The commission was directed to examine the constitution and rules in a comprehensive manner and to make any recommendations it considered necessary for the future development and administration of the association. The members were Chairman: James Nolan (director of fundraising); Secretary: Donal McGahon (regional chairman, St Kevin's region); Paul Ahern (director of development); Eric Curtis (Cloyne diocesan commissioner); Brian Doolan (Unit leader, 31st Dublin); Brig. Gen. Patrick D. Hogan (national executive board); and William James (Venturer leader, 49th Dublin). In its report, submitted in 1979, it provided an overview of the administrative history of the association, recalling that the first constitution was based on that of the Boy Scouts of America. One aspect of the US influence was the dominant position given to the troop committee which had sole charge of the leaders and boys. It also meant that scout leaders below the rank of commissioner could not be members of diocesan and national councils. In this constitution there was no mention of *Macaoimh Gasraí* (cub scout packs) or a programme for older boys in sea scouting, which were introduced in 1934 and 1936 respectively.

The report described the changes effected in the original constitution by the one published in 1957 as follows:

> A new constitution was introduced in 1957 which changed control of the troop from the troop committee to the troop chaplain. It also introduced a clear prohibition on scouters below the rank of commissioner being members of the national council, diocesan council and troop committee. It brought in the need for the approval of the bishop to start in a diocese and of the parish priest to start in a parish. In addition disputes within a troop were dealt with entirely by the clergy and not by the association.
>
> The constitution left matters relating to tests and uniform to be carried out by regulation.
>
> It still referred to troops only, although in practice the unit was the basic element of organisation and the provision of progressive training through the sections was being developed.
>
> The constitution introduced the need for amendments to be approved by the national council and subsequently by the hierarchy.

At the outset the review commission recommended that there be no change in the name of the association. One of the major issues considered by it was the admissibility of non-Catholics. It concluded:

(1) The CBSI is an association enjoying a special relationship with the Catholic Church.

(2) It is an association whose primary but not exclusive aim is to serve Catholics.

(3) It now considers itself to be an association which will admit persons satisfying conditions of the world scout movement.

In line with these considerations it proposed that appropriate changes be made in the constitution and rules.

The CBSI was organised in dioceses until 1970, when regions were introduced. For convenience sake the large Dublin archdiocese was divided into regions and in the north midlands smaller dioceses were joined to form a single region. The commission recommended that diocesan terminology should cease, that areas of the association should be known as regions and that the administrative structure should be national council – regional council – unit. On the vexed question of the control of each unit the review commission endorsed the existing rule: 'The unit council, with the unit leader, shall control the unit'. The commission recommended that where a unit did not have a chaplain this post be held by the appropriate regional chaplain or in the absence of such a chaplain it should be filled by the national chaplain, until a chaplain had been appointed. The importance of the charter was stressed. Its annual reception from the national executive board meant that a unit was a recognised element of the CBSI with a licence to take part in its programmes.

The review commission recommended the reduction of membership of the national council and sought to limit that of the national executive board to fifty. Recommendations were made with regard to directors and professional executives, the minimum age of those holding national offices, unit committees, trusteeship, accounts and commissioning. It advised that the scout salutation and patronal feasts be deleted from the constitution. The report of the revision commission was adopted and a further amended *Constitution and Rules* was prepared. However its publication was overtaken by events. By the mid-1980s leaders of the CBSI and SAI were discussing amalgamation and integration, not the new constitution.

ARCHBISHOP DERMOT RYAN

Archbishop Dermot Ryan was not as involved as his predecessor in the affairs of the CBSI. In 1973 he arranged with his Church of Ireland counterpart to bless and distribute shamrock on the reviewing stand of the GPO on St Patrick's Day. This ended a tradition of almost twenty years, wherein the chaplain of the 11th Dublin (Westland Row troop) blessed and distributed shamrock to the lord mayor and members of the troop each St Patrick's day. Archbishop Ryan was a firm supporter of the policy to update the CBSI and approved of its conversion from a diocesan to a regional structure.

REGISTERED NUMERICAL STRENGTH OF CBSI/CSI
The registered membership from 1959 to 2004 was as follows:

1959	4,242	1982	35,279
1960	5,502	1983	37,333
1961	4,811	1984	39,772
1962	5,562	1985	39,621
1963	5,467	1986	40,225
1964	6,891	1987	38,251
1965	8,088	1988	37,841
1966	8,603	1989	37,263
1967	8,715	1990	38,315
1968	9,000	1991	35,756
1969	10,296	1992	37,487
1970	11,020	1993	38,596
1971	12,000	1994	38,780
1972	13,000	1995	37,033
1973	14,410	1996	32,563
1974	15,217	1997	30,072
1975	18,080	1998	28,115
1976	21,440	1999	26,060
1977	24,234	2000	23,445
1978	27,745	2001	23,932
1979	28,951	2002	22,480
1980	31,905	2003	22,326
1981	34,620	2004	21,644

By contrast membership in the early years was much lower, standing at less than 2,000 in 1930, just over 3,000 in 1940 and slightly over 3,500 in 1950. Although there was a significant increase following the Eucharistic Congress in 1932, this was soon lost. The remarkable high rate of membership during the 1980s reflected, among other things, the rise in births in the 1960s. The steady decline in membership from the all-time high of 40,225 in 1986 to 21,644 in 2004 was caused by a number of factors, not least increased legal liabilities and the high cost of child protection policies. The following is a membership analysis by diocese in 1965:

	Total	Chaps	Cttes	Scouters	Boy scouts	Maca-oimh	Senior scouts	Knights
Achonry	nil	-	-	-	-	-	-	-
*Ardagh	42	1	7	3	31	-	-	-
*Armagh	330	4	25	17	172	91	21	-
Cashel	42	1	6	1	34	-	-	-
*Clogher	368	6	32	23	232	75	-	-
Clonfert	32	1	5	2	24	-	-	-
*Cloyne	140	2	12	7	69	42	8	-
*Cork and Ross	1,247	12	45	74	551	509	-	56
Derry	nil	-	-	-	-	-	-	-
*Down and Connor	430	8	22	31	196	173	-	-
*Dromore	127	3	13	6	84	16	5	-
*Dublin	3,701	44	171	223	1,723	1,261	218	61
Elphin	97	2	1	5	47	42	-	-
Ferns	91	1	5	6	30	42	5	2
Galway	94	2	12	9	52	14	-	5
Kerry	nil	-	-	-	-	-	-	-
Kildare and Leighlin	134	3	18	10	85	-	11	7
Killala	40	1	6	1	32	-	-	-
Killaloe	95	1	2	6	41	34	-	11
Kilmore	37	1	5	1	30	-	-	-
*Limerick	446	7	48	33	240	102	-	16
Meath	26	1	6	1	12	6	-	-
Ossory	96	2	4	4	77	-	9	-
Raphoe	nil	-	-	-	-	-	-	-
Tuam	38	1	8	1	28	-	-	-
*Waterford and Lismore	432	5	63	23	269	64	8	-
National Headquarters	3	-	3	-	-	-	-	-
Total	8,088	109	519	487	4,059	2,471	285	158*

(* Denotes diocesan councils) (*excluding knights holding commissions)

By 1965 only ten of the twenty-six dioceses – Ardagh, Armagh, Clogher, Cloyne, Cork and Ross, Down and Connor, Dromore, Dublin, Limerick and Waterford and Lismore – had diocesan scout councils. Subsequently there was a marginal increase in their number. About 45 per cent of CBSI membership belonged to the diocese of Dublin. In most years, however, the Dublin proportion of the entire membership was about 42 per cent and this proportion continued fairly constant throughout the rest of the history of the CBSI/CSI. It corresponded generally to the proportion of the Irish population that resided within and without the boundaries of Dublin diocese.

Derry had no scouts. It covered areas where republican sentiment and support was strong. For many years the senior clergy were cautious about promoting a disciplined organisation which might encourage boys to go on to join a more militant group. Ironically, when in the early 1970s grave civil unrest erupted in the Derry area, CBSI troops were established across the diocese of Derry with the obvious purpose of encouraging boys and young men to join them rather than Fianna Éireann or the Provisional IRA.

Kerry and Raphoe are listed as having no registered scouts. However, this did not mean there were no troops or scouts in these dioceses. For registration a troop needed to have its charter annually renewed and this was not done until after the appropriate application and registration fee based on membership was received by headquarters. Troops from time to time did not seek registration for financial or other reasons. And as most troops found it difficult to collect the weekly membership fee from many of their members, the vast majority of troops submitted only about two-thirds or less of their members. Thus the number of scouts in the country at any time would be at least 50 per cent greater than the number of registered scouts.

DEVELOPMENT OF LARCH HILL, 1938-2003
Following the formal opening of Larch Hill in 1938, five men were appointed to a committee to supervise the management of the national camp site, with one of them on duty each weekend. One who joined this group at a later date was consultant engineer, Nicholas Matthews, a member of the national executive board and of a troop committee. This Larch Hill committee was also charged with overseeing the development of the property. The immediate priority was to substantially improve the long entrance into the national camp site and to carry out essential major repairs on the main building which was in a state of serious disrepair.

As only meagre funds were available for rebuilding the house and improving the campsite, an appeal was made to senior scouts in the greater Dublin area to help with this work. Thereafter on weekends and summer evenings groups of senior scouts helped with the development of the site and with repairs on the house. In 1962 these groups and the committee supervising them became known as the *Meitheal*, an appropriate term which signifies a number of persons employed in cooperation on a specific task.

At the end of the 1950s an engineer's report stated that the old house at Larch Hill was in a dangerous condition. In 1965 it was abandoned and in the early 1970s demolished. Initially its role was provided by two wooden buildings, one of which was used as the training centre, the other as the premises for the '*Meitheal*' team. In 1968 it was decided to build a new training centre and hostel. Troops throughout the country were requested to raise funds for the purpose. This they did mainly by organising charity walks and other fundraising events. The resultant funds were generally divided equally between the charities in question, the local troop and the Larch Hill Building Fund.

In June 1972 the training centre and hostel was formally opened by President Éamon de Valera and afterwards Archbishop Dermot Ryan celebrated a thanksgiving Mass. The design of the new centre was supervised for the association by the director of property, Declan O'Driscoll, BE, and his predecessor, Paul Gibson, BE. The architects were John Thompson and partners of Limerick and Dublin. The centre included dormitories, meeting rooms and a kitchen area. Lieutenant Colonel Patrick D. Hogan, who was Chief Scout from 1970 to 1974, did not host the opening, as he had been called up to serve with the UN forces in Cyprus. His place was taken by the national commissioner, Stephen Spain, who, during Hogan's absence, acted as Chief Scout's deputy. Hogan, Spain, Donal McGahon, national secretary, and Dermot O'Mahony, national treasurer, were foremost in ensuring the successful completion of the new training centre.

In 1995 a new headquarters was built at Larch Hill with a grant of £400,000 from the department of the Taoiseach. Five years later the headquarters staff transferred to it from 19 Herbert Place, which was sold. At that time also the scout shop at 14 Fownes Street was transferred to 146 Capel Street, where it became a shop catering for scout requisites as well as equipment for outdoor activities. In 2003 the new headquarters, a pyramid-shaped building on the site of the former Larch Hill House, was formally opened as the national office of Scouting Ireland (CSI).

EUROPEAN EXECUTIVE COMMITTEE
After the affiliation of FISA to the World Scout Movement, the national secretary served on the committee for the European region of the World Scout
Movement. During Stephen Spain's membership between 1976 and 1979,
besides the need to enhance the education element in scouting and the
organisation of training programmes, one of the main topics discussed was
the restoration of scouting in Spain and Portugal following the end of the
Franco and Salazar regimes. The thrust of the committee was to try and
ensure conformity of policies and practices among the various national
scout organisations. Thus under its auspices the admission of girls to the
Irish scout organisation was facilitated. Already in the CBSI women and
girls had been leaders of cub packs since the early 1960s. Now in 1983 girls
were accepted as senior scouts and soon afterwards they joined the association at all levels.

PORTUMNA 1985, GOSFORD 1989
In the early 1980s the three scout associations in Ireland, CBSI, SAI and
NISC, agreed to jointly organise International scout camps at four-year
intervals and to site them alternately in the Republic and Northern Ireland.
Each association was, in turn, to take responsibility and act as host for these
events. The first was hosted by the SAI at Portumna, County Galway, in
1985. Michael Webb of SAI was camp chief. The camp was formally opened
by President Patrick Hillery. It was most successful with over 10,000 scouts
participating. The next camp was hosted by the body that had been the governing authority for B-P scouts in Northern Ireland since 1987, the Scout
Association of Northern Ireland (SANI), at Gosford Forest Park, near
Markethill, County Armagh, in 1989. The camp received considerable
media coverage when visited by the Duke of Kent, president of the Scout
Association of the UK.

BALLYFIN 1993, LOUGH DAN 1997
The third jointly-organised camp was held under the auspices of the CBS1,
in the grounds of the Patrician College at Ballyfin, County Laois, from 27
July to 5 August 1993. The aims set out for the camp were: (1) 'to enable a
significant number of scouts to have a truly international experience and (2)
to build on the cooperation and spirit of Portumna '85 and Gosford '89'.
Kiernan Gildea was camp chief. He was assisted by three deputy camp
chiefs. One of these was George Purdy. Appointed chief commissioner of
Northern Ireland a year later, in 1996 he became Chief Scout of the UK

Scout Association. Most Irish troops were represented among the 7,000 who camped at Ballyfin. There were also contingents from Australia, Canada and fifteen European countries. The camp was formally opened by President Mary Robinson with Sir Patrick Mayhew, secretary of state for Northern Ireland, and other distinguished visitors in attendance.

The next Camp was at Lough Dan, near Roundwood, County Wicklow, in 1997. Hosted by the SAI, it did not generate the same support as previous ones, with just 2,000 scouts attending it. SANI made extensive preparations for a Camp at Castle Archdale, near Belleek, County Fermanagh, in 2001. The project, however, had to be abandoned, owing to the serious outbreak of foot and mouth disease. Since then a number of factors have militated against organising these camps. There was the preoccupation of leaders at national level with preparations for the integration of the two scout associations. Another serious obstacle was the high costs of organising them. These have been considerably inflated by increasing charges for adequate insurance cover against personal injury claims.

SCOUTING AS USUAL, 1980-2005

Scout groups followed their programmes throughout the country. Apart from organising Irish international scout camps, Ireland's scouts were represented at the World Scout jamborees: in Kananaskis Country, Alberta, Canada, in 1983; Catarack Scout Park, New South Wales, Australia, in 1987; Mt Sorak National Park, Seoul, South Korea, in 1991; Flevoland, Holland, in 1995; Picarquin, Santiago, Chile, in 1999; and Sattahip, Thailand in 2003. Woodbadge training courses to promote competence in leadership and scoutcraft continued. The mountain pursuit challenge to encourage mountain hiking was inaugurated in 1991. The Phoenix Challenge replaced the competition for the Melvin trophy in 2005. The outlets for scout uniforms and equipment were reorganised in 2005, with two in Dublin, at Liffey Street and Middle Abbey Street, and one in Cork at McCurtain Street.

At national level scout leaders were completing preparations for the integration of the two associations. This was agreed in principle in 1998. After widespread consultation final decisions on outstanding issues were taken in October 2002 and May 2003. Scouting Ireland (SI) was agreed in June 2003 and it was formally established by members of CSI (formerly CBSI) and SAI on 1 January 2004. The first meeting of the new association's national council was held in October 2004. Its mission statement indicated that the new association provided for Catholic, Jewish, Moslem or Protestant units, also mixed units with members from some or all of these religious faiths. It emphasised that the overriding consideration was that the rules and programmes of each group were based on the traditions, ideals and aims of the scout movement, as it had evolved over almost a hundred years. SI had a membership of 30,725, with CSI providing 21,644 and SAI 9,081. (For details on membership figures for 2003 and 2004, see Appendix 3). Formal recognition of the new association was obtained from the World Organisation of the Scout Movement (WOSM). Uniformity in practice and terminology was encouraged throughout the new association. All local formations were termed groups and the association was structured on a provincial and county basis. A new uniform, consisting of a dark-blue shirt and dark-blue slacks, was introduced on 1 August 2005. All that remained was for the scouts, including their leaders, to get back as one on the 'scouting trail'.

LETTER FROM PATRICK HUGHES, NATIONAL SECRETARY,
CBSI, TO FR WILLIAM D. HAMILTON, SCOTTISH NATIONAL
CATHOLIC SCOUT CHAPLAIN, DATED 24 OCTOBER 1956

Dear Father Hamilton,

It was a great pity your letter of 8 October arrived here the day I left for London on my longest business trip for some years and that you have had to wait such a length for my reply.

Your queries may, I think, be best answered by question and answer form as follows:

1) *What does CBSI claim to be?*

   The only association in Ireland with authority to promote the methods, principles and exercises of scouting among the Catholic boys of Ireland.

2) *Who alone has the power to give such authority?*

   The archbishops and bishops of Ireland.

3) *Who gave that authority to CBSI?*

   The Irish Hierarchy after their meeting held in Maynooth in June 1926.

4) *Has any other body in Ireland authority or approval to educate Catholic boys through scouting?*

   No other association has such authority or even tacit approval from the Irish Hierarchy.

5) *How is CBSI organised throughout Ireland?*

   Entirely on a diocesan basis, with each bishop's nominee as diocesan chaplain in control of Catholic scouting in each diocese.

6) *Has this type of organisation affected CBSI's international relationship?*

   Yes. The dioceses of Ireland do not conform with or follow the political boundary. The primitial diocese of Armagh, for instance, crosses the political border and comes down to within thirty miles of Dublin. As CBSI refuses to confine its operations and its organisation within the limits of political boundaries, the International Bureau cannot grant affiliation.

7) *Has any other reason been advanced by the International Bureau for its non-recognition of CBSI?*

No other reason has been advanced by either Colonel Wilson, General Spry or Mr Lund.

8) *Does the International Bureau know the above facts?*

The International Bureau knows all the above facts and is completely aware that CBSI caters for the Catholic 94 per cent majority of the population and that the other Scout association can do little else than cater for the scouting needs of the other 6 per cent of the population.

9) *Is there any possibility that CBSI will restrict its activities to the 26 counties of Southern Ireland in order to secure recognition by the International Bureau?*

I cannot, of course, speak for the future but it is highly improbable that CBSI would wish to relegate its members in Northern Ireland into an association under British control. It is also highly improbable that CBSI would seek to divorce itself from active cooperation with the bishops of Ireland for the sake of international recognition. So far, therefore, as I can visualise the position there is no possibility that CBSI would so restrict its activities. All members of CBSI believe that the partition of Ireland is entirely unnatural and we can, therefore, afford to wait for the day when we shall have a united country.

10) *How is Ireland represented at official scout international conferences?*

All European Catholic countries are represented at official scout international conferences by Catholic delegates. Ireland, a 94 per cent Catholic country, has for years been 'represented' by a non-Catholic who cannot speak either with authority or knowledge of the needs or wishes of the people or their children. This farcical situation must be a source of embarrassment both to the International Bureau and to the Irish association which claims in international circles what it dare not claim in Ireland – to be representative of the nation.

Some other questions may spring to your mind and I need hardly tell you that I shall be glad indeed to clarify the situation for you.

With every good wish and my regret that this reply has had to be so long delayed.

Yours sincerely,
Patrick Hughes

APPENDIX 2

MEMORANDUM OF THE PROPOSAL FOR
THE FORMATION OF A
FEDERATION OF IRISH SCOUT ASSOCIATIONS

The Background: International scouting is organised through the World Scout Committee operating the World Scout Bureau located at Ottawa, Canada. Over eighty countries, with a total scout membership of 9,365,000 are affiliated. This body arranges or supervises international jamborees and conferences, international leader training programmes and representation on international organisations, UNESCO etc. By the rules of the World Scout Committee only one body can be affiliated in any country. In the Republic the affiliation is held by Boy Scouts of Ireland (B-P scouts) and in the Six Counties by the Boy Scout Association, London, which controls B-P scouting in these countries.

The Present Situation: The Catholic Boy Scouts of Ireland Association has been invited by the World Scout Committee to become affiliated to the world body.

The Method: To achieve the affiliation of CBSI, the recognition now accorded to the Boy Scouts of Ireland would have to be relinquished by them and transferred to another body of which Boy Scouts of Ireland and Catholic Boy Scouts of Ireland were both members. This is necessary because of the rules of the World Committee referred to above (1). The formation of such a joint body for recognition purposes is the method by which the problem has been overcome in those many countries where more than one scout association exists. The suggestion is naturally acceptable to the World Scout Committee, is acceptable to the Boy Scouts of Ireland and to the Boy Scout Association, London.

The Advantages: There are two major advantages which would arise from such affiliation:
(1)   CBSI members could take part in the international events arranged by the World Bureau, thus ensuring a more true representation of Irish scouting and a more Catholic influence at these gatherings.

(2)   Through CBSI membership Catholic influence in the international councils of scouting would be strengthened.

(3)   In addition, the federation could provide the opportunity of representing Irish scouting in possible discussion with government or other bodies on technical, practical or financial questions.

The Safeguards: The constitution of the proposed federation would be most carefully prepared to ensure that the federation would exist for recognition purposes only and have no function or power in the internal affairs of the member association which would remain autonomous and independent as heretofore.

The following points would be included:

(1)   The membership to consist of BSI and CBSI represented by not more than 5 members from each body. (CBSI would probably be represented by the Chief Scout, national chaplain, national secretary, national treasurer and international commissioner.)

(2)   The chairmanship and other offices to rotate every two years between the two member associations.

(3)   Funds: Expenses to be met, and income (if any) shared by the member associations according to an agreed formula (e.g. a half divided equally and a half in proportion to registered membership).

(4)   All decisions shall be taken in unanimous vote.

(5)   Provision for change in the constitution of the federation, only by unanimous agreement.

APPENDIX 3

Scouting Ireland Membership figures for 2003 and 2004

Northern Province

	Beavers	Cubs Scout/Macaoimh	Scouts	Venturers	Total Youths	Adults
CSI	722	943	718	75	2,458	597
SAI	193	219	106	4	522	119
SI Total	915	1,162	824	79	2,980	716

Southern Province

	Beavers	Cubs Scout/Macaoimh	Scouts	Venturers	Total Youths	Adults
CSI	1,229	1,569	1,379	180	4,357	976
SAI	287	400	204	22	913	154
SI Total	1,516	1,967	1,583	202	5270	1130

Western Province

	Beavers	Cubs Scout/Macaoimh	Scouts	Venturers	Total Youths	Adults
CSI	445	726	542	44	1,757	445
SAI	250	263	138	6	657	129
SI Total	695	989	680	50	2,414	574

North Eastern Province

	Beavers	Cubs Scout/Macaoimh	Scouts	Venturers	Total Youths	Adults
CSI	506	743	669	138	2,056	456
SAI	602	1,107	494	42	2,245	322
SI Total	1,108	1,850	1,163	180	4,301	778

South East Province

	Beavers	Cubs Scout/Macaoimh	Scouts	Venturers	Total Youths	Adults
CSI	837	1,171	919	96	3,023	695
SAI	483	816	385	13	1,697	284
SI Total	1,320	1,987	1,304	109	4,720	979

Dublin Metropolitan Province

	Beavers	Cubs Scout/Macaoimh	Scouts	Venturers	Total Youths	Adults
CSI	780	1,355	1,402	355	3,892	932
SAI	257	731	654	77	1,719	320
SI Total	1,037	2,086	2,056	432	5,611	1,252

Scouting Ireland Total Membership

	Beavers	Cubs Scout/Macaoimh	Scouts	Venturers	Total Youths	Adults
	6,591	10,043	7,610	1,052	25,296	5,429

	Beavers	Cubs Scout/Macaoimh	Scouts	Venturers	Total Youths	Total adults
CSI 2004	4,519	6,507	5,629	888	17,543	4101
CSI 2003	4,581	6,718	5,863	907	18,069	4,257
SAI 2004	2,072	3,536	1,981	164	7,753	1,328
SAI 2003	2,120	3,662	2,371	186	8,339	1,657

	Total Youth	Total Adults
CSI 2003	18,069	4,257
CSI 2004	17,543	4,101
SAI 2003	8,339	1,657
SAI 2004	7,753	1,328

2003-2004 TOTALS

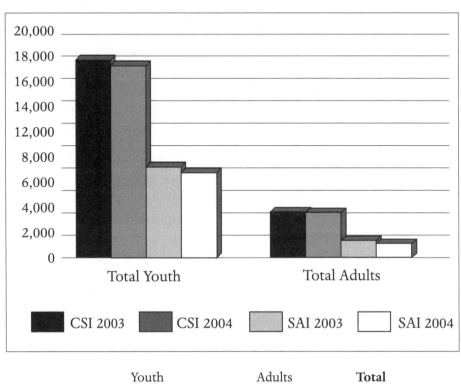

	Youth	Adults	Total
CSI2003	18,069	4,257	**22,326**
CSI2004	17,54	4,101	**21,644**
SAI2003	8,339	1,657	**9,996**
SA12004	7,753	1,328	**9,081**
SI 2004	25,296	5,429	**30,725**

Baden Powell on scouting in his own words and drawings

ABOUT THOSE BOY SCOUTS

Has it ever struck you that you ought to be connected with them ?

But you ought to be if only for your own amusement, because there's lots of fun and also a lot of good to be got out of it. "Got out of it," yes — and before you've been

Who? —
ME - a Boy Scout ? !!

in it five minutes a strange thing happens : instead of looking to see what you are going to get out of it you are looking to see what you can put into it.

Are you , in a general way. efficient ! Of course you are , you can read and write and so on and — Yes , well , for instance — can you swim ?

Yes, of course you can   and can box a man of your own weight or hold off an attack by a ju-jitsu grip?

Can you carry your own golf clubs and stalk your own stag — or do you need a fellow to do it for you?

Can you catch a fish and milk a cow, and light a fire and cook your own food on occasion, or must you starve because you are dependent on some one else 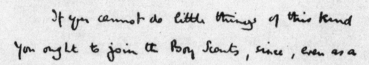 to do these simple things for you?

Do you know how to stop a runaway horse, or rescue a drowning person, or to render First Aid in the case of a cut artery?

If you cannot do little things of this kind you ought to join the Boy Scouts, since, even as a

'grown-up' you will there learn them fast enough.
If, on the other hand, you can already do them it is
equally important for you to join the Scouts —
in order that you may impart the knowledge to the
boys.

Of course you may say that you are too old or much
too busy, or not quite strong enough, or that you
don't understand the variety of subjects that a
Scoutmaster has to know. These are the
objections advanced by 9 out of 10 of our workers
before they joined and before they found themselves
up to the neck — heart and soul — in it, in spite
of them. Or possibly you are a lady

It doesn't matter.

The fact is whoever you are and whatever you are
it is in your power to do something for the boy.
That sounds a big order but it is a fact.

you have a hobby of some sort

The boys are just aching for hobbies.
You can probably draw a sketch or
mend a clock or collect butterflies.
We need instructors in every kind of direction, if only
for an hour or two a week. Can you not spare that
amount of time ?

If you are too old you will find that
mixing with the boys makes you young
again: age exchanges its experience for
the fresh young dreams of boyhood.
[And old 'uns can at any rate generally
help with funds]
The number of invalids whom Scouting
has led to forget their ills is very large.
The Scoutmaster does not need to be an Admirable
                                        Crichton....

Yours truly

Baden Powell

From Baden-Powell to today: the spirit of scouting

DONAL McGAHON[1]

T HE 'EDWARDIAN SUMMER' of pre-1914 Britain is a memory suffused with constant sunshine and balmy breezes. Britain seemed to rule most of the world although there had been a recent unpleasantness with the Boers. They had been seen off with the aid of heroes such as Colonel Robert Baden-Powell.

Boys in Edwardian Britain led dull lives, either at school or leaving school early to work in dead-end jobs. Their dress would have been knickerbockers suits, topped off with a school-type cap. The quality, cut and general condition of the boys' clothing indicated social class. However it was a generation which was almost entirely literate thanks to the spread of primary education.

Imagine the excitement when it was announced that Baden-Powell or B-P had written a book called *Scouting for Boys*. The first of the six fortnightly parts appeared on 15 January 1908 and despite its high price of four pence was snapped up everywhere.

The small booklet had an exciting cover by noted poster artist John Hassall. It showed a boy dressed casually in a shirt and shorts, with a staff and a B-P hat beside him. The boy was peeping cautiously around a boulder at a group on a beach doing mysterious things at the water's edge with an ominous ship on the horizon.

The book was a rag-bag of ideas, stories of adventure, heroics and moral worth with lots of new things to try out and activities for your gang,

---

1 Donal McGahon has served at all levels of scouting including a period as national secretary of the CBSI. He is a holder of the Order of Cuchulain, SI's highest merit award.

which B-P called a 'patrol'. There were also games, one of which was 'played in the 21st Dublin Company Boys' Brigade'.

B-P explained how you could set up your own patrol and if there was more than one patrol, then these would form a troop. The old cavalry terms came in handy. Each patrol would be about eight boys, just about the size of a gang, and one of the scouts would be the patrol leader. Adults would be useful as leaders or instructors.

To be a scout you had to accept some rules by which you would live your life. These were set out in the scout promise and law. Membership also had to be voluntary.

The book created a sensation and very soon thousands of boys were out trying the exercises and activities that B-P had suggested. They adapted their clothing to resemble the illustrated scout uniform. Adults began to notice this activity and many offered their assistance in running troops. In many cases it was a case of mutual approaches between local boys and adults.

In contemporary terms the casualness of their dress and the independence of their activities were startling in such a rigid society. But in other ways this made it even more popular amongst those boys to whom scouting appealed.

The new patrols and troops followed B-P's suggestions as to organising their activities. Younger scouts were taught the skills of scouting by the older scouts, retiring patrol leaders were replaced by other patrol members and soon there were badges for proficiency in special skills. These badges could be worn on a uniform sleeve.

The emphasis was on outdoor activities, especially hiking and camping. The range of activities and the fact that the boys themselves were involved in deciding what was to be done, even when there were adult leaders, contributed greatly to its sweeping success. It very soon eclipsed the existing youth organisations of the Boys' Brigade (for whom the scheme had originally been designed) and the Cadet Corps.

Scouting for Boys Part 1 is an amazing document. In its seventy pages of 'Campfire Yarns' is outlined the essential scheme of scouting with its educational basis and structure at boy level.

It was to be adapted for different countries, for girls, and for different age-groups and has influenced an estimated 350 million members to date. The original ideas of B-P have now been refined into the scout method which is formalised as follows:

Scouting achieves its aim through a system of progressive self educa-tion, known as the scout method, the principal elements of which are:

1. Voluntary membership of a group which, guided by adults, is increas-ingly self-governing in its successive age groups.

2. Commitment to a code of living as expressed in the promise & law, the meaning of which is expanded as the member grows towards maturi-ty.

3. The provision of opportunities for leadership and responsibility.

4. Learning by doing.

5. Encouragement of activity in small groups.

6. An award scheme, which encourages participation in its full range of activities and provides recognition of individual and group achieve-ments.

Chief Scouts

1

CUMANN GASÓGA NA HÉIREANN/SCOUT ASSOCIATION OF IRELAND

1908–1941	Lt-Gen Robert Stephenson Smyth Baden-Powell
1941-1945	Lord Somers
1945-1949	Lord Rowallan
1949-1965	Lord Powerscourt
1966-1973	Ernest Judge
1973-1980	Commodore Thomas McKenna
1980-1984	Joseph McGough S.C.
1984-1991	Eoghan Lavelle
1991-1997	Kenneth Ramsey
1997–2004	Donald Harvey

GASÓGA CATOILICÍ NA HÉIREANN/CATHOLIC BOY SCOUTS OF IRELAND

1927–1930	Senator John O'Neill
1930–1962	Professor Joseph B. Whelehan
1962–1970	Christopher J. Murphy
1970–1974	Brig-Gen Patrick D. Hogan
1974–1980	James D. Hally
1980–1986	Joseph Lawlor
1986–1992	Paul Ring
1992–1998	Joseph Lawlor
1998–2004	Peter Dixon

GASÓGA NA HÉIREANN/SCOUTING IRELAND

2004–	Martin Burbridge

2

FIANNA ÉIREANN

1909–1910	Bulmer Hobson (president)
1910–1915	Countess Constance Markievicz (president)
1915–1916	Pádraig Ó Riain (Ard Taoiseach)
1917–1918	Countess Constance Markievicz (Chief of Na Fianna)

1918–1919	Éamonn de Valera (Chief of Na Fianna)
1919–1922	Countess Constance Markievicz (Chief of Na Fianna)
1924–1927	Countess Constance Markievicz (Chief of Na Fianna)
1927–1931	George Plunkett (Ard Taoiseach)
1932	Frank Ryan (Ard Taoiseach)
1933–1940	George Plunkett (Ard Taoiseach)
1955–1958	Conleth O'Kelly (Ard Taoiseach)
1958–1959	Frank Leigh (Ard Taoiseach)
–1991	Brian Keating (Ard Taoiseach)
1992–	Kevin Braney (Ard Taoiseach)

3
UK SCOUTS IN NORTHERN IRELAND

1908–1941	Lt-Gen Robert Stephenson Smyth Baden-Powell
1941–1944	Lord Somers
1945–1959	Lord Rowallan
1959–1971	Sir Charles Maclean
1972–1982	Sir William Gladstone
1982–1988	Maj-Gen Michael J. Walsh
1988–1996	Garth Morrison
1996–2004	George Purdy
2004–	Peter Duncan

Sources

PART 1

A

Unpublished
Dublin, Scouting Ireland, National Campsite, Larch Hill, Tibradden.
   Connell, John, Typescript: 'History of B-P scouts in Southern Ireland: 1908-1958'.
Dublin, Dr Eoghan Lavelle, 50 Beech Park Drive, Foxrock.
   Typescript: 'History of B-P sea-scouting in Ireland.'

B

Published
Aitken, W.P., *The Chief Scout, Sir Robert Baden-Powell* (London 1912).
Baden-Powell, Robert, *The Matabeland campaign* (London 1896).
_____, *Scouting for boys* (London 1908).
_____, *The Wolf Cub's handbook* (London 1916).
_____, *Aids to scoutmastership* (London 1919).
_____, *Rovering to success* (London 1922).
Baden-Powell, Warington, *Sea-scouting and seamanship for boys* (London 1912).
Bell, Margaret, *A history of scouting in Northern Ireland* (Belfast 1985).
Collis, Henry: Hurll, Fred: Hazlewood, Rex, *B-P's scouts: an official history of the Boy Scouts Association* (London 1961).
Drewery, Mary, and Baden-Powell, Olave, *Window on my heart* (London 1973).
Dublin Boy Scouts' Association: *Annual Reports* 1946, 1947, 1948, 1949, 1950, 1953, 1959.
Evening Herald, 'Scout notes' (weekly col.), July 1962-June 1964.
Evening Mail 20 March 1909; 29 August 1914; 'Boy scout news' (weekly col.) 1949-1950; January 1957-1960.
Freeman's Journal 16 August 1915.

Hillcourt, William, *Baden-Powell, the two lives of a hero* (London 1964).

Irish Times, 'Youth movements' (weekly col.) 1959-1963.

Irish scouting news, October 1970 to April 1975.

Jamboree: journal of world scouting, December 1954.

James, Dermot, 'Potted history', *Irish scouting news*, October 1970.

_____, *The purple scarf* (Dublin 1990).

Jeal, Timothy, *Baden-Powell* (London 1989).

McGrath, Walter, *CBSI: 50 years agrowing* (Dublin 1977).

Scout headquarters gazette, September 1915.

Sunday Times 12 June 2005.

The Boy Scouts Association: *Policy, organisation and rules* (London 1947).

The Boy Scouts' headquarters gazette: Irish supplement, May 1920-August 1921.

The Irish scout 1937-39.

The Jamboree book 1920 (London 1920).

World scouting, February 1957.

Young, Robert E., *First steps in scouting* (Glasgow 1940).

C

Persons

Gillespie, Kenneth, Northern Ireland Scout Council, 109 Old Milltown
    Park, Belfast, BT8 75P.

James, Dermot, 22 Nutgrove Park, Dublin 14.

Kiely, Terence, 31 Glenlucan, Killarney Road, Bray, County Wicklow.

Lavelle, Dr Eoghan, 50 Beech Park Drive, Foxrock, Dublin 18.

Webb, Michael J., 2 Mount Salus, Dalkey, County Dublin.

D

Film

Dublin, Irish Film Archive, Irish Film Institute, 6 Eustace Street.

Crawford Collection: includes scout camps: Powerscourt 1927 and 1928
    and Chief Scout's visit to Powerscourt, August 1928.

PART 2

A

Unpublished

Dublin, Archdiocesan Archives, Holy Cross College, Clonliffe.
   Papers of Archbishop John Charles McQuaid.
Dublin, Archives Department, University College.
   Denis McCullough Papers.
      P120/24 (9, 10, 13).
      P120/28(4).
      P120/76.
Dublin, Military Archives, Cathal Brugha Barracks, Rathmines.
   Bureau of Military History 1913-21

Witness Statements

Bevan, Séamus; member of FÉ 1916; Witness Statement (WS) 1058, 1059.
Brady, Liam; officer FÉ, Derry 1920-22; WS 676.
Brennan, Lt Col Seán; officer FÉ and IRA, Dublin 1918-24;
      Contemporaneous Document (CD) 316.
Busby, James Allan; lieutenant FÉ, Cork 1921; WS 1628.
Cashin, Séamus; officer FÉ, 1909-16; WS 8.
Christian, William; member FÉ, 1911; member IV, Dublin 1916; WS 646.
Daly, Patrick, see under O'Daly.
Doyle, John; member FÉ, Dublin 1921; CD 315.
Dwyer, Thomas; member FÉ, Enniscorthy; member IV 1915-1919; officer
      IRA and flying column Wexford, 1919-1921; WS 1198.
Fulham, Comdt James; member FÉ 1916; member IRA, Dublin 1921; WS
      630.
Harling, Sean; officer FÉ 1921; courier, Dail Éireann 1920-21; WS 935.
Healy, Sean, Barrack St, Cork, officer FÉ, Cork 1916; WS 47.
Hearne, Comdt Patrick; FÉ, Waterford 1921; WS 1742.
Hensy, Comdt M.; member FÉ, Tullamore 1916; WS 13.
Hobson, Bulmer; member supreme council IRB 1915; general secretary IV
      1916; founder FÉ 1902 (Belfast) and 1909 (Dublin); WS 53, 81, 82, 83,
      84, 85; CD 8, 38, 41.
Holland, Robert; member IRB, FÉ and IV 1909-1916; member IRA, Dublin
      1917-1921; WS 280, 371; CD 147.

Holohan, Garry; senior officer FÉ 1914-1921; WS 328, 336; CD 135, 156.

Hurley, George; member FÉ, Cork 1917-21; WS 1630.

Kilmartin, Michael; member FÉ, County Clare 1920-21; CD 144.

Langley, Liam; officer FÉ, Dublin 1921; WS 816.

Lonergan, Michael; officer FÉ, Dublin 1909; WS 140.

Lynskey, William; member FÉ, Dublin 1919-21; WS 1749.

Martin, Eamon; senior officer, FÉ 1912-21; WS 591, 592, 593; CD 238.

Meaney, Charles; captain FÉ, Cork 1917-21; WS 1631.

Mundow, Henry J.; officer FÉ, Dún Laoghaire 1921-1923; CD 325.

Murphy, John C.; member FÉ 1917; member IV and IRA, Cork 1919-1923; WS 1217.

_____, Kevin; lieutenant FÉ, Cobh 1921; WS 1629.

_____, Comdt P.J.; captain FÉ, Cork, 1912-16; WS 869.

MacNeill, Maj Gen Hugo; commandant FÉ, Dublin 1919-1921; WS 1377.

_____, Col Niall; son of Eoin MacNeill; officer FÉ 1916; officer IV and IRA, South Dublin 1919-21; WS 69.

McCabe, William (Liam); captain FÉ, Kerry 1921; WS; 1212.

McCarthy, Mrs Cathleen; sister of Pádraig Ó Riain, one of the founders of FÉ; WS 937.

Nolan, James; officer FÉ, Waterford 1921; WS 1369.

O'Callaghan, Liam; officer FÉ, Cork 1916; WS 47.

O'Connell, Patrick; member FÉ, Limerick 1916; WS 329.

O'Connor, Thomas; officer FÉ, Kerry 1921; WS 1189.

O'Daly, Maj Gen Patrick; lieutenant FÉ 1913-16; lieutenant IV, Dublin 1913-16; member ASU, 1920-21; WS 220, 387.

O'Grady, Charles J.; member FÉ and IV, 1913-16; WS 282.

O'Leary, Michael; commandant FÉ, Kerry 1921; WS 1167.

O'Riain, Pádraig; general secretary FÉ, 1909-16; WS 98.

O'Sullivan, Dermot; member FÉ 1913; IRA, Dublin 1921; ASU, 1921; WS 508.

Pelican, Thomas; captain FÉ, Kerry 1918; WS 1109.

Pounch, Séamus; captain FÉ, Dublin 1916; assistant quartermaster general FÉ, 1920-21; WS 267-294.

Prendergast, Seán; member FÉ 1911; officer IV, Dublin 1914-16; captain IRA, Dublin 1921; WS 755;802.

Reidy, Amos; member FÉ, IV and IRA, Limerick 1917-21; WS 1021.

Reynolds, Joseph; senior officer FÉ, 1914-21; WS 191.

Rowan, James; member FÉ, Dublin 1913-14; Post Office telegraph messenger 1916; WS 871.

Saunders, Seán; captain FÉ, 1917-1920; adjutant Dublin brigade, FÉ, 1920-
21; courier, department of local government, Dáil Éireann, 1919-21;
WS 817, 854.

Ward, Patrick; formation FÉ, Dublin 1909; member IV and IRA, Dublin
1914-21; WS 1140.

White, Alfred; QMG, FÉ, 1921; WS 1207.

Contemporaneous Documents

29, Group 4, FÉ Belfast.

50, Group 3, *Fianna Handbook*.

62, Group 13, *Fianna*.

91, Group 2, FÉ organising, fund and photographs 2, 4 and 5.

144, Group 1, Na Fianna Éireann 1030x.

258 Group 5, Na Fianna Éireann 1 and 2.

Dublin, National Library of Ireland, Kildare Street.

MS   5760.
5770.
10910.
12176.
12177.
12178.
12179.
13771.
18817.
22113.
33571.
33700.
35455.

Dublin, Anthony C. Coughlan, Social Studies Department, Trinity
College.

Belfast 1969-70: some misconceptions corrected.

('This commentary seeks to set the record straight as to the respective roles of Anthony Coughlan, Roy Johnston and the late C.
Desmond Greaves in the political development that culminated in
the outbreak of violence in the Six Counties of Northern Ireland in
1969-70.')

Sources

B
Published

An Claidheamh Soluis 14, 21 August 1909; November 1913.

Bean na hÉireann (The women of Ireland) November 1908 – September 1910.

Doyle, Jennifer, Clarke, Frances, Connaughton, Eibhlís, Somerville, Orna, *An introduction to the Bureau of Military History 1913-1921* (Dublin 2002).

Evening Herald 3, 7 March 1962.

Evening Press 20 September 1968.

Fianna, February 1915-April 1916; 1924.

Fianna Éireann 1 August 1991-1 May 1992.

Fianna Éireann handbook (Dublin 1909, repr. 1914).

Fianna Éireann handbook (Dublin 1914).

Freeman's Journal 15 July, 21 October 1913.

Gaelic American 14 April to 16 June 1917.

Gaughan, J. Anthony, *Listowel and its vicinity* (Cork 1973).

Greaves, C. Desmond, *Liam Mellows and the Irish revolution* (London 1971).

Hay, Marnie, 'This treasured island: Irish nationalist propaganda aimed at children and youth, 1910-1916', *Treasure islands,* ed by Mary Shine Thompson and Celia Keenan.

Herlihy, Jim, *The Dublin Metropolitan Police: a short history and genealogical guide* (Dublin 2001).

Hickey, D.J., and Doherty, J.E., *A new dictionary of Irish history from 1800* (Dublin 2003).

Hobson, Bulmer. *Ireland yesterday and to-morrow* (Tralee 1968).

Holland, Robert, *A short history of Fianna Éireann* (Dublin 1992).

Irish Freedom, November 1910-December 1914.

Irish Nation 19 June 1909.

Irish Times 1 August 1913; 29 March 1966.

Irish Volunteers, February 1914- April 1916.

James, Dermot, *The Gore-Booths of Lissadell* (Dublin 2004).

Larkin, Emmet, *James Larkin, Irish labour leader 1876-1846* (London 1965).

Lawlor, Caitriona (ed), *Seán McBride, That day's struggle: a memoir 1904-51* (Dublin 2005).

MacEoin, Uinseann, *Survivors* (Dublin 1980).

_____, *The IRA in the twilight years* (Dublin 1997).

MacFhloinn, Pádraig, *Fianna Éireann handbook: Lámhleabhar Fianna Éireann* (Dublin 1988).

MacLeod, David, *Building character in the American boy: the boy scouts, YMCA and their forerunners* (Madison 1983).

Marreco, Anne, *The rebel countess: the life and times of Countess Markievicz* (London 2000).

Neeson, Eoin, *Birth of a Republic* (Dublin 1998).

Nodlaig na bhFiann, December 1909; December 1914.

O'Farrell, Padraic, *Who's who in the Irish war of independence and civil war* (Dublin 1997).

Ó Seaghadha, Donnchadh (ed), *The Irish boy scouts by Liam Mellows* (reprinted from *Gaelic American* with introduction and notes (Dublin 2001).

O'Shannon, Cathal (ed), *Souvenir of the golden jubilee of Fianna Éireann* (Dublin 1959).

O'Toole, Fintan, *The Irish Times book of the century* (Dublin 1999).

Sisson, Elaine, *Pearse's patriots: St Enda's and the cult of boyhood* (Cork 2004).

Skinnider, Margaret, *Doing my bit for Ireland* (New York 1917).

The constitution of Na Fianna Éireann (Dublin 1909, amended in 1912).

The Phoenix 2 December 2005 ('Pillars of Society': Séan Garland).

The young guard of Erin (Fianna Éireann handbook) (Dublin 1964).

Van Voris, Jacqueline, *Constance de Markievicz in the cause of Ireland* (Dublin 1967).

PART 3

A

Unpublished

Dublin Archdiocesan Archives, Holy Cross College, Clonliffe.
   Papers of Archbishop Edward Byrne.
   Papers of Archbishop John Charles McQuaid.
   Papers of Archbishop Dermot Ryan.
   Register of priests.

Dublin, Scouting Ireland, National Campsite, Larch Hill, Tibradden.
   Ballyfin '93 international scout jamboree: final report.

Dublin, John Graham, 30 Shanowen Park.
   Conversation between Jim Hally and George Shaw, Northern Ireland, on the start of the Catholic boy scouts in Belfast.

Dublin County, Donal McGahon, Larch Hill, Tibradden..
   Notes on CBSI origins.

Report of the Constitution Review Commission 1979.
Tipperary. County, Archdiocesan Archives, St Patrick's College, Thurles.
    Register of priests.
Waterford, County Heritage Museum at Mount Mellery Scout Centre, Cappoquinn.
    Brief account of Belfast Catholic boy scouts.
    Brief history of Limerick scouting 1928 to 1980.
    History of the first pilgrimage to Rome of the Catholic boy scouts of
    Ireland: March 7th-24th 1934 by Scout Paddy Ryan – 1st Kilkenny.

B

Published
A think in time (Dublin 1944)
Bolster, Evelyn, *The Knights of St Columbanus* Dublin 1979).
Boy scout's camp book (Dublin 1944).
Bree, Tommy, Manning, Brian, Vaughan, Michael, Ward, Brian, *The scouting
    trail, official handbook of CBSI* (Dublin 1979).
Constitution and Rules of CBSI (Dublin 1957).
_____ , (Dublin 1970).
Corrigan, Patrick W., *Ki-Ro handbook* (Birmingham 1955).
Dáil Éireann reports 1919-1923.
Duggan, Phil (ed), *Fifty years of Abbeyside scouting* (Waterford 1980).
Encyclopaedia Britannica (London 1957), under Boy Scouts and Boy Scouts of
    America.
Fenby, Jonathan, *The sinking of the Lancastria* (London 2005).
Handbook of organisation and rules (Dublin 1943).
How to run a troop (Dublin 1944).
Investiture ceremonial (Dublin 1943).
Irish Catholic 28 November 1925; October 1927.
Irish Catholic directory (Dublin).
Irish Independent 4 November 1968.
Irish Monthly, February 1932.
Is your son a scout? (Dublin 1944).
Kavanagh, Colm *The scouting trail, a field book for scouts* (Dublin 2003).
_____, Joe, *Looking back on St Peter's scouts* (Belfast 2004).
Kerryman 10, 31 July, 7 August 1958.
Lee, Jack, *Early days of the CBSI movement in Cork city* (Cork 1980).
Letters to a scoutmaster (Dublin 1943).
McGahon, Donal, *CBSI ceremonies* (Dublin 1979).

McGahon, Donal and MacMahon, John, *Come scouting* (Dublin 1963).
_____, *The scouting trail* (Dublin 1965).
McGrath, Walter, *Fifty years agrowing: pictorial history of Catholic boy scouts of Ireland* (Cork 1979).
Martin, Colbert, *A drink from Broderick's well* (Dublin 1980).
My cub scout adventure (Dublin 1985).
O'Sullivan, Damien, *A brief history of Larch Hill* (Dublin 2002).
Our Boys 28 May-17 August, 1 October, 12, 26 November 1925; 7 January, 15, 19 April 1926; 8 March-25 May; 9 June; 23 June-18 August, 15 September 1927. (Brother Allen Library, Edmund Rice House, North Richmond Street, Dublin 1.)
Scouting for Catholics (Dublin 1943).
Scouting Ireland: code of good practice (Dublin 2005).
Scout leader 1959-2001.
Silver jubilee 1928-1953: Gasóga Catoilicidhe na hÉireann: Limerick diocese (Limerick 1953).
The Catholic Scout, November 1932.
The Catholic scout leaders' bulletin 1943, 1944 and 1945.
The Catholic scout movement (Dublin 1942).
The Leader 5, 12 December 1925.
Troop committee work (Dublin 1943).
Why be a boy scout? (Dublin 1944).

C

Persons

Burbridge, Martin, 'Westwood', Derryvarogue, Donaghdee, Naas, County Wicklow.
Carroll, Colman, 78 Manor Street, Dublin 7.
Cullinane, Walter, 4 Glen Lawn Drive, The Park, Cabinteely, Dublin 18.
Fahy, Mrs. Charlotte, 20 Rockville Drive, Blackrock, County Dublin.
Fehily, Mgr G. Thomas, 4 Eblana Avenue, Dún Laoghaire, County Dublin.
Gildea, Kiernan, 28 Temple Court, Palatine Square, Dublin 7.
Graham, John, 30 Shanowen Park, Dublin 9.
Greene, Mgr Stephen, 97 Kincora Avenue, Clontarf, Dublin 3.
Hally, James, 'The Burgery', Abbeyside, Dungarvan, County Waterford.
Kennedy, Fr Bernard, 57 Edenvale Road, Dublin 6.
Kennedy, John O'Loughlin, 28 Proby Square, Blackrock, County Dublin.
Kennelly, Matthew, Cloth Hall, Listowel, County Kerry.

Sources

Kiely, Dominick, 220 Ballinacurra Gardens, Limerick.

Kincaid, Malcolm, 40 Fernhill Park, Dublin 12.

McGahon, Donal, Scouting Ireland, National Campsite, Tibradden, County Dublin.

McGrath, Walter, 5 Ferncliffe Villas, Bellevue Park, Cork.

MacMahon, Canon John, The Presbytery, Putland Road, Bray, County Wicklow.

Matthews, Fr Colm, 47 Old Court Manor, Dublin 24.

O'Connor, Séamus, 24 Abbey Park, Blackrock, County Dublin.

Price, Fr Cathal, 54 Foxfield St John, Dublin 5.

Rogers, David, 27 Pheasant Walk, Collins Avenue, Dunmore Road, Waterford.

Spain, Stephen, 131 Richmond Court, Dublin 6.

D

Film

Dublin, Scouting Ireland National Campsite, Larch Hill, Tibradden.
    Irish Movietone: Catholic boy scouts pilgrimage to Rome 1934.

Dublin, Irish Film Archive, Irish Film Institute, 6 Eustace Street.
    'Campa': activities of an encampment of boy scouts 1942.

E

Website

There is an enormous number of scout websites. Many are run by individuals and some are not safe. Two are properly maintained and supervised, that of the World Organisation of the Scout Movement (WOSM) and of Scouting Ireland (SI). The former is www.scout.org, the latter is www.scouts.ie.

Index

Handbook 44, 52
Field Company of Collins'
  Barracks 137
*Fifty years agrowing: pictorial history
  of the Catholic Boy Scouts of
  Ireland* (book) 96
Figgis, Darrell (gun-runner) 47
Findlater Place (Dublin) 37
Fine Gael (party) 59, 137
Finnegan, Fr Thomas 136
Fitt, Gerry (nationalist leader) 72
Fitzgerald, Theo (FÉ) 51
Fitzmaurice, Col James (aviator) 95
  John (scoutmaster) 95
Fitzwilliam Square (Dublin) 105
Flevoland (Holland) 146
Foley, A. (scoutmaster) 94
Forde, OMI, Fr 136

Fortune, Lieut R.P. (founder of 1st
  Dublin troop) 5, 8
Four Courts (Dublin) 56-8
Fownes Street (Dublin) 127, 144
France (country) 11, 21, 104, 113-4,
  126, 137
Franciscan College (Gormanston)
  129
Franco, General (dictator) 145
Freemasons 84, 129
French, Field Marshal Viscount 13
Lord Mayor Seán 96
  bayonets' 38, 44
Friend, General (OC, Brit. forces in
  Ireland) 11
Frongoch (prison camp in Wales)
  51
Gaelic American (newspaper) 41
  Athletic Association (GAA) 33-4,
  52
  League (Conradh na Gaeilge) 33,
  36, 40
Gaiety Theatre (Dublin) 110

Gallagher, Fr Dan 106, 109-12, 127,
  133-5; see ill. 35
Galway (county) 50, 82, 99, 114,
  137, 145
Garda Síochána 61, 70, 74, 117
  Special Branch 61, 74
'Garden Plots Scheme' 11
Garland, Seán (IRA) 65
General Strike and Lock-out 1913,
  9
Geneva (Switzerland) 5
George V (king) 7, 40
Germany (country) 20, 47, 126
Gibraltar (port) 102
Gibson, Paul (engineer) 144
Gildea, Kiernan (scout leader) 145;
  see ills. 45, 46
Gilwell Park (London) 8, 24, 96, 98,
  113, 122-3
Gladstone, Sir William (Chief
  Scout,UK scouts) 163
Glandore (Cork) 82
Glasgow (Scotland) 4, 39
Glasnevin (Dublin) 29, 48, 52
  cemetery 52, 73, 107
Glenavy, Lord 15
Glendon, OP, Fr 83
Glenstal Abbey (Murroe) 123
Glynn, Sir Joseph A. 84, 89
Godollo (Hungary) 18
Gold, Lt Col R. 132
Good Friday Agreement 73-4; see
  also Belfast Agreement
Gore-Booth, Constance 35; see also
  under Markievicz
Gorey (Wexford) 44
Gorman, Fr Enda 121, 128-30, 133,
  138; see ill. 36
Goulding, Cathal (IRA) 65, 67, 69
Gormanston (Meath) 129
Gosfort Forest Park (Markethill) 145